FOREWORD

This publication has been prepared under our direction for use by our respective commands and other commands as appropriate.

JOHN N. ABRAMS
General, U.S. Army
Commanding General
U.S. Army Training and Doctrine
    Command

J. E. RHODES
Lieutenant General, USMC
Commanding General
Marine Corps Combat
    Development Command

B. J. SMITH
Rear Admiral, USN
Commander
Navy Warfare Development
    Command

LANCE L. SMITH
Major General, USAF
Commander
Headquarters Air Force
    Doctrine Center

This publication is available on the General Dennis J. Reimer Training and Doctrine Digital Library at
www.adtdl.army.mil

PREFACE

1. Scope

This publication is a tactical level document for planning and conducting aviation urban operations. This publication—

- Supplements established doctrine and tactics, techniques, and procedures (TTP).
- Provides reference material to assist aviation and ground personnel in planning and coordinating tactical aviation urban operations.
- Applies to any personnel planning and conducting aviation urban operations, including commanders, planners, aircrew, and ground personnel requiring aviation support.
- Promotes an understanding of the complexities of urban terrain.
- Incorporates lessons learned, information from real world operations and training exercises, and TTP from various sources applicable to the urban environment.

2. Purpose

This publication provides multiservice TTP (MTTP) for planning and executing fixed- and rotary-wing aviation urban operations.

3. Applicability

a. The audience for this publication is any element of a force planning and conducting aviation urban operations, including commanders, planners, aircrew, and ground personnel requiring aviation support. This publication can serve as a source document for developing Service and joint manuals, publications, and curricula, as supplementary documentation or as a stand-alone document.

b. This publication does not address all functions of airpower employment that may be used in urban operations (e.g. counterair, strategic attack, air interdiction, etc.), as these topics are addressed in other appropriate joint and Service publications.

4. Implementation Plan

Participating Service command offices of primary responsibility (OPRs) will review this publication, validate the information, reference, and incorporate it in Service and command manuals, regulations, and curricula as follows:

Army. The Army will incorporate this publication in United States (US) Army training and doctrinal publications as directed by the Commander, US Army Training and Doctrine Command (TRADOC). Distribution is in accordance with Department of the Army (DA) Form 12-99-R.

Marine Corps. The Marine Corps will incorporate these procedures in US Marine Corps (USMC) training and doctrinal publications as directed by the Commanding General, US Marine Corps Combat Development Command (MCCDC). Distribution is in accordance with the Marine Corps publication distribution system (MCPDS).

Navy. The Navy will incorporate these procedures in US Navy (USN) training and doctrinal publications as directed by the Commander, Navy Warfare Development Command (NWDC). Distribution is in accordance with the military standard requisitioning and issue procedure (MILSTRIP) Desk Guide and naval standing operating procedure (NAVSOP) Publication 409.

Air Force. The Air Force will validate and incorporate appropriate procedures in accordance with applicable governing directives. Distribution is in accordance with Air Force instruction (AFI) 33-360.

5. User Information

a. The TRADOC-MCCDC-NWDC-Air Force Doctrine Center (AFDC)-Air Land Sea Application (ALSA) Center developed this publication with the joint participation of the approving Service commands. ALSA reviews and updates this publication as necessary.

b. This publication reflects current Service and joint doctrine, command and control (C2) organizations, facilities, personnel, responsibilities, and procedures. Changes in Service protocol, appropriately reflected in Service and joint publications, will be incorporated.

c. We encourage recommended changes for improving this publication. Key your comments to the specific page and paragraph and provide a rationale for each recommendation. Send comments and recommendation directly to one of the following services:

Army

Commander
US Army Training and Doctrine Command
ATTN: ATDO-A
Fort Monroe VA 23651-5000
DSN 680-3153 COMM (757) 727-3153

Marine Corps

Commanding General
US Marine Corps Combat Development Command
ATTN: C42 (Director)
3300 Russell Road, Suite 318A
Quantico VA 22134-5021
DSN 278-6234 COMM (703) 784-6234

Navy

Commander
Navy Warfare Development Command
ATTN: N5
686 Cushing Road
Newport, RI 02841-1207
DSN 948-4201 COMM (401) 841-4201

Air Force

HQ Air Force Doctrine Center
ATTN: DJ
216 Sweeney Boulevard Suite 109
Langley AFB VA 23665-2722
DSN 574-8091 COMM (757) 764-8091
E-mail Address: afdc.dj@langley.af.mil

ALSA

ALSA Center
ATTN: Director
114 Andrews Street
Langley AFB, VA 23665-2785
DSN 575-0902 COMM (757) 225-0902
E-mail: alsa.director@langley.af.mil

FM 3-06.1
MCRP 3-35.3A
NTTP 3-01.04
AFTTP(I) 3-2.29

FM 3-06.1	US Army Training and Doctrine Command Fort Monroe, Virginia
MCRP 3-35.3A	Marine Corps Combat Development Command Quantico, Virginia
NTTP 3-01.04	Navy Warfare Development Command Newport, Rhode Island
AFTTP(I) 3-2.29	Headquarters Air Force Doctrine Center Maxwell Air Force Base, Alabama

15 April 2001

AVIATION URBAN OPERATIONS
Multiservice Procedures for
Aviation Urban Operations

TABLE OF CONTENTS

Page

EXECUTIVE SUMMARY

Aviation Urban Operations

This publication–
- Provides MTTP for tactical level planning and execution of fixed- and rotary-wing aviation urban operations.
- Provides reference material to assist aircrew and ground personnel in planning and coordinating tactical urban operations.
- Applies to all elements of a force planning and conducting aviation urban operations, including commanders, planners, aircrew, and ground personnel requiring aviation support.
- This publication does not address all functions of airpower employment that may be used in urban operations (e.g. counterair, strategic attack, air interdiction, etc.), as these topics are addressed in other appropriate joint and Service publications.

Chapter I
Overview

Chapter One provides an overview of aviation urban operations including lessons learned to show effective and ineffective techniques. This overview includes discussion of political and civilian considerations, law of war, rules of engagement, and collateral damage considerations. The chapter also addresses the importance of fratricide prevention measures.

Chapter II
Urban Characteristics

Chapter Two describes characteristics of urban terrain including size, patterns, and features. It describes building construction, building types, street patterns, roof coverage, population density, and other features of special consideration.

Chapter III
Flight Operations

Chapter Three includes discussions concerning threat considerations, effects of weather, command, control, and communications, and airspace control considerations. The chapter includes information on aviation capabilities and employment limitations. It discusses night vision devices, urban navigation, landing zone selection, and other flight operations considerations unique to aviation urban operations.

Chapter IV
Weapons Employment

Chapter Four focuses on tactical urban targeting, and weapons selection. It discusses target marking devices, friendly unit position marking, laser designation, and positive control measures. The information provided includes aerial weapons effects, ordnance delivery parameters, target tracking, and emergency close air support considerations.

PROGRAM PARTICIPANTS

Joint

Joint Warfighting Center Fenwick Rd Bldg 96, Fort Monroe, VA 23651-5000
HQ JSSA, Fort Belvoir, VA
HQ JCRA, Langley AFB, VA
Joint Combat ID Office (JCIDO), Washington, DC
HQ USSOCOM (SOOP-J/SORR-SCG), MacDill AFB, FL 33621-5323

Army

HQ TRADOC (ATDO-A), Ingalls Rd, Bldg 133 Room 7, Fort Monroe, VA 23651-5000
Combined Arms Center (CAC), Combined Arms Doctrine Directorate (CADD), Fort
    Leavenworth, KS
US Army Infantry Center, Fort Benning, GA
CDR USAFAS, Fort Sill, OK
CDRUSAAVNCS, DOTDS, Fort Rucker, AL
101st Airborne Division (AASLT), Fort Campbell, KY
10th Mountain Division (Light), Fort Drum, NY
160th Special Operations Aviation Regiment (Abn)

Marine Corps

Marine Corps Combat Development Command, Joint Doctrine Branch (C427), 3300
    Russell Rd, 3rd Floor Suite 318A, Quantico, VA 22134-5021
HQ US Marine Corps Stategy and Plans Division, Room 5D 616, Washington, DC
    20380-1775
Marine Aviation Weapons and Tactics Squadron One (MAWTS-1), P.O. Box 99200,
    Yuma, AZ 85369-9200
Second Marine Aircraft Wing, Cherry Point, NC

Navy

Navy Warfare Development Command/Det N3, 1540 Gilbert Street, Norfolk, VA 23511
Naval Strike and Air Warfare Center (NSAWC), Fallon NAS, NV
COMPHIBGRU TWO, NAB Little Creek, Norfolk, VA 23521

Air Force

HQ Air Force Doctrine Center, 155 N. Twining Street, Maxwell AFB, AL 36112
AFDC Detachment 1, 216 Sweeny Bvld. Ste 109, Langley AFB, VA 23665
HQ ACC/ XOIP/XODT, Langley AFB, VA 23665
HQ AMC/DO/DOK/XP/DOKT, Scott AFB, IL 62225
HQ USAF/XPXQ/XOOC, Washington DC
HQ USAFE/XPXD, Ramstein AFB, GE
HQ AFSOC/DO/DOXT/IN, Hurlburt Field, FL
USAFWS/WSR/WST, Nellis AFB, NV
AC2ISRC/C2S, Langley AFB, VA
57 WG/DTW, Nellis AFB, NV
AWFC/422 TES/CC/DOA, Nellis AFB, NV
720 STG/CC, Hurlburt Field, FL

Chapter I
OVERVIEW

1. Introduction

a. Background. Urban areas generally function as centers of social, economic, industrial, and political power. These areas facilitate formal and informal civilian and military interaction, and can offer ready access to important resources, such as labor, water, technology, and information. Historically, United States (US) Forces have operated within, or in close proximity to urban areas. Demographic and population trends indicate that, in the future, a majority of the world's population will reside in urban areas. Trends toward increased urbanization increase the potential for US forces to operate in urban areas.

b. Doctrine. US Army and US Marine Corps (USMC) doctrine recommends isolating and bypassing urban areas when possible due to the costs involved. Former Soviet Union doctrine also recommended avoiding large cities in favor of speed and maneuver. However, avoiding urban areas does not prevent an adversary from exploiting its defensive advantages. US Air Force (USAF) doctrine maintains that airpower's versatility and responsiveness allows the simultaneous application of mass and air maneuver, almost anywhere, from almost any direction. The speed, range, precision weapons, communications, command and control (C2), information gathering, and transportation capabilities of US military aircraft enable airpower to play a major, if not decisive, role in urban operations when proper tactics are employed. This is possible whether aviation operations are conducted independently, or in conjunction with the operations of friendly ground forces. Operations in Panama City, Baghdad, Mogadishu, Port Au Prince, Sarajevo, and Pristina, are a few examples where airpower has been influential in urban operations in the past.

c. Urban Considerations. Aviation urban operations can be planned and conducted across the range of military operations. The two dominant characteristics affecting aviation urban operations are the existence of manmade construction and the presence of noncombatants. These operations may be conducted on or against objectives on a complex urban topology and its adjacent natural terrain. The compressed battlespace in the urban environment creates unique considerations for planning and conducting aviation operations. These include:

(1) operations in urban canyons,

(2) deconfliction in confined airspace,

(3) restrictive rules of engagement (ROE),

(4) difficulty in threat analysis,

(5) an overload of visual cues,

(6) the presence of noncombatants,

(7) the potential for collateral damage, and

(8) the increased risk of fratricide.

These considerations and others, as well as some historical lessons will be discussed in this publication.

2. Historical Lessons

a. Background. Urban operations have been conducted many times in the 20th century. See Table I-1. Familiarity with historical lessons is fundamental to understanding the difficulties associated with conducting aviation urban operations. In many conflicts throughout the 20th century, aviation (air power) has played an important and sometimes decisive role in isolating and interdicting the flow of the defender's supplies and reinforcements into the urban areas. Advancements in aircraft design and precision munitions in conjunction with specific training for urban operations have increased effectiveness of these operations. For example, the Israel Defense Forces (IDF) during operations in Beirut, successfully used aviation in a compressed urban battlespace through bombing by fixed-wing aircraft, ground attack by helicopters, and aerial medical evacuation of wounded personnel.

b. Tactical Challenges. Employment of aviation assets in urban operations presents important tactical challenges. For example, one tactic used successfully by both attackers and defenders for protection against air and artillery attack has been to keep one's forces deployed in close proximity to the enemy; thus deterring enemy air or artillery support. This "hugging" tactic, whether by design or as a consequence of close combat, was often effectively used in many modern urban battles.

c. Planning and Conducting Operations. Due to the complexities and increased challenges involved in conducting aviation urban operations, the following are some of the important areas of consideration when planning for and conducting operations in this environment.

(1) Physical limitations. Urban areas offer defenders several advantages. These include the availability of obstacles, cover, concealment, and potential strongpoints. City layouts limit traditional methods of military operations. The vertical nature of this environment and subterranean infrastructure limit line of sight (LOS).

(2) Surprise. Surprise can help shift the balance of combat power by overcoming other disadvantages and may be critical to success in urban operations. Surprise was achieved by the attacker at Aachen and Ban Me Thout and by the defender at Suez City. Without the element of surprise, friendly forces may encounter strong, well-prepared defenses without adequate warning. Rapid, accurate, intelligence analysis and dissemination is a key to the element of surprise.

Table I-1. 20th Century Urban Operations

EBROIN	1938	WARSAW	1939
ROTTERDAM	1940	MOSCOW	1942
STALINGRAD	1942	LENINGRAD	1942
WARSAW	1943	**PALERMO**	**1944**
TOKYO	**1944**	DRESDEN	1944
BREST	**1944**	WARSAW	1944
AACHEN	**1944**	ORTONA	1944
CHERBOURG	**1944**	BRESLAU	1945
WEISSENFELS	**1945**	BERLIN	1945
MANILA	**1945**	**SAN MANUEL**	**1945**
BERLIN AIRLIFT	**1948-49**	**SEOUL**	**1950**
BUDAPEST	1956	**BEIRUT**	**1958**
SANTO DOMINGO	**1965**	**SAIGON**	**1968**
KONTUM	**1968**	**HUE**	**1968**
BELFAST	1972	MONTEVIDEO	1972
QUANGTRI CITY	**1972**	**AN LOC**	**1972**
XUAN LOC	**1975**	**SAIGON**	**1975**
BEIRUT	**1975-78**	MANAGUA	1978
SIDON	1982	KABUL	1978-87
TYRE	1982	**PANAMA CITY**	**1989**
KHAFJI	**1991**	**BAGHDAD**	**1991-98**
MOGADISHU	**1992-94**	PORT AU PRINCE	1994
SARAJEVO	**1994-98**	GROZNY	1994-95
MONROVIA	**1996**	**FREETOWN**	**1997**
BELGRADE	**1999**	PRISTINA	1999
NOTE: Bold type denotes direct US involvement			

(3) Isolation. Sustained isolation of a defending force has often afforded the attacker a tremendous combat advantage. Conversely, minimizing or overcoming the effects of isolation has often enabled victory by defending forces. The offensive use of airpower by the attacking force has often significantly influenced the isolation of defending forces by stemming what could otherwise be an unimpeded flow of manpower, supplies, and weapons to replace their losses. The battle at Khafji is one example, where, during fierce ground fighting in and around the city, coalition air forces destroyed Iraqi reinforcements from the air. However, airpower's influence on isolation is not limited to aerial bombardment. For example, the employment of airlift and special operations aircraft has helped attacking forces initiate and/or sustain attacks to isolate defending forces by massing friendly ground troops into urban areas. Operations in Panama City and Port Au Prince are two examples where this was the case. Additionally, airpower has also helped defending or occupying friendly forces and populations in urban areas overcome the effects of isolation through resupply and humanitarian relief efforts, such as operations in Berlin, Mogadishu, and Sarajevo.

(4) Time. In most cases, the time required for successful conclusion of an urban operation exceeded the initial estimates. Two operations where time played a critical role in the attacker's strategic timetable (and this role was not anticipated) were Aachen and Stalingrad. In these operations, the defenders delayed the

attackers longer than was estimated, resulting in the modification of operational or strategic plans. A well-planned urban defense, even if the defender is isolated or lacking aviation, armor, or artillery, can consume inordinate amounts of the attacker's time and resources. This time can permit the defender to reorganize, redeploy, or otherwise effectively marshal resources in other areas.

(5) Intelligence. Many defeats can be attributed to errors in the initial intelligence assessments. The operation at Arnhem in World War II might not have occurred if the Allies had been aware of the strength and locations of the German forces. At Stalingrad, the attacking Germans were aware of the defending forces facing them in the Sixth Army's zone. However, they incorrectly analyzed the build-up of Soviet forces in *other* areas; thus resulting in tactical surprise at those points, and diluting their offensive to seize the city. Aviation forces are uniquely suited to provide timely, thorough, and on-demand intelligence, although the urban environment poses some unique challenges to aerial and space reconnaissance.

(6) Forces. Whether attacking or defending, the size of the force relative to the enemy's can be a critical determinant of success or failure. Historically, when the attacker outnumbered the defender and/or the quality of defending forces was inferior, the defeat of the force defending the city was almost certain. The average attacker to defender ratio in the battles referenced in Table I-1 was four-to-one. Nevertheless, regardless of the size or quality of the defensive forces, the defender can exact enormous costs on the attacker in time, resources, and casualties. As was seen at Khorramshahr, the defensive Iranian forces, which were outnumbered four to one, still held the city for approximately twenty-six days. Another consideration for both attacker and defender is the inversely proportional relationship between force strength and combat duration. Historically, the stronger the attacker, the shorter the duration of the fight. Aircraft and their unique capabilities provide a significant force multiplier to either an attacker or defender.

(7) Command, Control, and Communications (C3). C3 is often difficult in the urban environment. In particular, controlling airspace and air to ground coordination may be hampered by physical and technical limitations. The urban environment may adversely affect friendly-force communications, with LOS communications severely limited at times. Effective communications requires planning and clear orders.

(a) Planning must address redundant and alternate means of communications. Visual signaling, while difficult, has proven to be effective when other means of communication are unavailable. The use of commercial telephone systems or landlines may be also appropriate, but are susceptible to damage, sabotage, and monitoring. Airborne platforms or rooftop retransmission systems can help alleviate these problems by providing the "high ground" for communications relay. The IDF for example, employed unmanned aerial vehicles as retransmission platforms during the War in Lebanon (1982) with considerable success. In addition to enhancing operations by serving as communications relays, airborne platforms may also provide commanders real or near-real time intelligence.

(b) There is always the possibility some subordinate units may be out of contact with higher headquarters during much of their mission execution. Therefore, clear orders to subordinate commands, and a thorough understanding of the commander's intent is essential in helping subordinates understand the larger context of their actions. This allows them to exercise judgement and initiative When situations change, making a task obsolete, an understanding of intent is more lasting and continues to guide subordinate commanders' actions. General Chuikov of the 62nd Russian Army summed up the concept of commander's intent when speaking of the battle of Stalingrad: "Fighting in a city...is much more involved than fighting in the field. Here, the 'big chiefs' have practically no influence on the officers and squad leaders commanding units and subunits and into those of the soldiers themselves."

(8) Weather. Weather may adversely affect aviation operations. Over-reliance on aviation forces may render a force, particularly in the high intensity environment of urban combat, susceptible to the uncertainties of weather. In the battle for Hue City for example, US Marines were unable to effectively employ aviation because of low cloud ceilings. Consequently, only one flight of A-4s was able to employ ordnance in support of the Marines fighting in Hue City during the entire battle.

(9) Logistics and medical. Urban operations require a responsive logistical support system. Of particular importance is a responsive and robust treatment and evacuation plan for casualties. To meet casualty and evacuation needs, plan to establish aid stations and landing zones as far forward as the situation allows.

(10) ROE. Because aviation urban operations normally pose a high risk of civilian collateral damage and fratricide, operations-specific ROE must be crafted carefully to allow flexibility in fulfillment of the mission. At the same time, ROE must limit the danger to noncombatants and friendly forces. Because this is such a crucial issue in the context of urban operations, some historical examples are instructive.

(a) Manila–1945. Before the battle of Manila in 1945, General MacArthur prohibited aerial bombardment. "The inaccuracy of this type of bombardment would result beyond question in the death of thousands of innocent civilians." He further confined artillery support to observed fire on confirmed point targets. However, the artillery restrictions were removed after the first few days because of growing US casualties. Furthermore, in apparent disregard for the ROE, cases of air bombardment and strafing in support of US forces occurred in the latter stages of the battle. During this operation, much of the city was destroyed, or damaged and an estimated 100,000 civilians died.

(b) Seoul–1950. At the outset of the battle, US Marines entered the fight under very restrictive ROE. Both damage to the city and civilian casualties were to be held to a minimum. There was to be no close air support (CAS) at all. However, this restriction was lifted in the face of heavy enemy opposition. In the aftermath of the US victory over the defending North Korean forces, 65% of the city was destroyed and thousands of South Korean civilians were killed.

(c) Hue City–1968. As US Marines entered Hue City in 1968, the use of heavy artillery, bombs, and napalm was prohibited. The Army of the Republic of Vietnam corps commander's request to spare civilians and reduce destruction to the historic city drove these restrictions. However, as the battle's progress slowed with significant US Marine casualties, this policy was abandoned and artillery and tanks became a crucial factor in the ultimate success of the battle. In the aftermath of the US victory over the defending North Vietnamese forces, "the estimates tallied ten thousand houses either destroyed or damaged, roughly forty percent of the city."

3. Political and Civilian Considerations

a. Collateral Damage. One of the risks in urban operations is the possibility of widespread collateral damage. While this damage is unintended, the resulting images of destroyed homes, damaged churches, and injured civilian casualties may have severe operational consequences. This damage is exacerbated by world wide media reports and enemy attempts to characterize such damage as unlawful. These media reports and claims may affect strategic decision making and lead to the loss of international and public support. Commanders and planning staffs must keep these considerations in mind at all times when planning or conducting urban aviation operations. One of the ways in which these issues can be managed is through the careful drafting and management of ROE. However, paramount to the drafting of these ROE is the need to emphasize the right and obligation of self-defense, force protection, and military necessity.

b. Military/Civilian Interaction. During urban aviation operations, US forces should expect that many civilians and civilian objects would be intermingled with military objectives. Some civilians will pose risks because they may be hostile to US Forces. This may involve civilians committing hostile acts against US or friendly forces. On the other hand, the majority of civilians will act strictly in accordance with their status as non-combatants. Non-combatants should be protected and respected at all times. Therefore, efforts must be made to protect non-combatants and civilian objects, which by definition are not military objectives. Military objectives are those objects, which by their nature, location, purpose, or use effectively contribute to the enemy's war fighting or war sustaining capability. However, the will of the population can be targeted by non-violent measures including offensive information operations (IO). IO can persuade civilians to avoid any involvement in combat operations. IO can also inform non-combatants of the likely location of combat operations. This information assists them in avoiding any accidental involvement, and in minimizing the likelihood of incidental injuries. However, these kinds of IO should be consistent with operations security (OPSEC) requirements and fully integrated with other IO actions.

c. Post-Hostilities Support. After hostilities cease, military forces may be required under international law to take on the burden of providing support to the civilian population in any occupied territory until civilian authority is restored. Accordingly, commanders must keep in mind that destruction of essential urban infrastructure can complicate this post combat transition period. Therefore, air planners and commanders conducting aviation urban operations must be mindful of all the issues associated with civilian presence.

4. Law of War (LOW)/Law of Armed Conflict (LOAC)

It is US policy that our forces will abide by LOW/LOAC in all their military operations, no matter how characterized. Urban aviation operations present unique challenges, but these too must be conducted in compliance with LOW/LOAC. Commanders and planners must seek the advice of judge advocates at all stages of planning to ensure compliance with LOW/LOAC. The two most fundamental and important LOW/LOAC concepts are *distinction* and *proportionality*.

a. *Distinction*.

(1) The concept of distinction requires that combatants make every effort to distinguish between military targets and civilian persons or objects. The principle of distinction prohibits intentional attacks on non-combatants or non-military objects. Urban operations require accurate targeting, precision weapons, and realistic training to distinguish successfully between military and civilian targets.

(2) It is extremely important to distinguish between non-combatants and combatants. This task can be greatly complicated by the urban environment. Valid military targets or combatants belong to any of the following categories:

(a) members of armed forces,

(b) members of organized militia,

(c) members of resistance movements,

(d) inhabitants of a non-occupied area who take up arms on the approach of the attacking force,

(e) any civilian who actively poses a direct threat to US forces,

(f) any structure that produces services or warfighting equipment for the fighting force.

(3) In urban areas, it is often impossible to distinguish adequately between combatants and non-combatants or between military targets and civilian objects. LOW/LOAC attempts to ameliorate this dilemma by requiring defending forces to remove the civilian population from the vicinity of military objectives and not to locate military objectives within or near densely populated areas. Although strictly prohibited by LOW/LOAC, recent experience demonstrates that defenders may attempt to render military forces and objectives immune from attack by mixing their soldiers among non-combatants and using civilian structures for overtly military purposes. A failure by an adversary to adequately safeguard the civilian population does not relieve the attacking commander from his obligation to consider civilian collateral damage and injury—any attack must still be *proportionate*.

(4) US forces will face similar dilemmas in future operations. When an unscrupulous enemy uses members of the civilian population as "human shields", US forces are under no legal obligation to assume all responsibility for their safety, nor to place US lives at undue risk. While US forces may attack lawful targets consistent with the principle of proportionality, the enemy may exploit civilian casualties resulting from their use of human shields. Therefore, commanders should be prepared to provide information to counter enemy misinformation.

b. *Proportionality.*

(1) The concept of proportionality requires that any application of combat power against a lawful military target and any resulting damage to noncombatant life and/or property not be disproportionate to the military advantage anticipated. For example, under most circumstances leveling an entire city block to kill a single sniper is disproportionate.

(2) The concept of proportionality as applied to the high population density urban environment implies the need for weapons with precise and controllable effects. Particularly in the urban environment, excessive weapons effects can result in disproportionate civilian collateral damage.

5. Rules of Engagement

a. Background. Drafting and implementing ROE is a challenging but vital issue when planning and executing urban operations. As in any operation, ROE must be liberal enough to allow commanders operational flexibility while ensuring friendly forces stay within the mission's legal, political, and operational boundaries. Although tension exists between operational efficiency and necessary constraints in all ROE, the close proximity and intermingling of civilian persons and objects in the urban combat environment greatly magnifies this tension. When drafting air ROE, this problem is even more acute. Careful consideration must be given to weapon system capabilities and C3 assets when crafting air ROE for the urban environment. The degree of positive control of air assets and surety of target identification that is both desirable and possible must be carefully considered.

b. Developing ROE. During planning, ROE must be carefully drafted and thoroughly reviewed in the context of scenarios likely to be encountered by friendly forces—"chair flying" and "what-iffing" is essential at this time. Operational planners should seek guidance and advice from legal and civil affairs (CA) personnel to ensure proposed ROE are consistent with LOW/LOAC, national directives, and the mission's political mandate. During deployment and execution, commanders must continually evaluate the ROE and make recommendations for modifications as required by mission exigencies. The ROE must be practical, realistic, enforceable, flexible, and clearly stated. Chairman of the Joint Chiefs of Staff (CJCS) standing ROE (SROE) found in CJCS Instruction (CJCSI) 3121.01A, and other applicable theater ROE must be analyzed and incorporated during planning.

c. ROE Guidance. LOW/LOAC and the SROE provide authoritative guidance when drafting operation-specific ROE. With SROE, a system is in place to ensure authoritative ROE guidance at all times, and to develop mission specific rules. Units must ensure that the ROE are available and conduct periodic ROE training.

d. Publish and disseminate ROE to all levels. Commanders must ensure training facilitates a thorough understanding of the ROE by all members of the force. When the ROE changes, there must be a system established to ensure the changes are disseminated and implemented. Mission rehearsals should include ROE exercises during which individuals apply the ROE in realistic situations. Remember, failure to comply with ROE is punishable under the uniform code of military justice (UCMJ) and may in extreme instances constitute a war crime, so commanders have a moral obligation to ensure all their personnel are thoroughly familiar with mission ROE.

6. Collateral Damage

Collateral damage is the unavoidable or unplanned damage to civilian personnel or property resulting from an attack on a military target. An important fact to keep in mind is that civilian collateral damage is *not* illegal under LOW/LOAC; *excessive* civilian collateral damage is. Generally, the incidental loss of civilian life or damage to civilian property must not be excessive relative to expected military damage to be gained from the attack. This is the concept of *proportionality* in military attacks. During urban operations, civilian collateral damage may be significant, and the goal should be to minimize collateral damage and the inherent risk to non-combatants to the greatest extent possible under the circumstances. The risk to non-combatants can be mitigated by:

a. appropriate weapon selection,

b. carefully drafted ROE,

c. positive tactical control of offensive air assets, thorough training in urban tactics,

d. moving non-combatants to a safer location whenever possible.

7. Fratricide Prevention

a. Background. Fratricide is the employment of friendly weapons and munitions with the intent to kill the enemy or destroy his equipment or facilities, which results in unforeseen and unintentional deaths or injury to friendly personnel. Fratricide prevention is a matter of concern in all operations. In urban operations, the characteristics of the terrain create an environment posing additional challenges. The challenge is minimizing fratricide without unreasonably restricting the friendly force's ability to accomplish the mission. Reducing fratricide requires accurate information pertaining to the location of friendly, neutral, and hostile personnel. This is facilitated through our training, doctrine, tactics, techniques, and procedures (TTP), C3, and sensor employment.

b. Fratricide Potential. Urban terrain increases the potential for fratricide because of the likelihood of close quarters, location and identification (ID) problems, and unintentional secondary weapons effects. During operations in Panama City in Operation JUST CAUSE, infantry units operating in limited visibility participated in a coordinated attack with aviation assets. Smoke resulting from preparatory fires began to obscure much of the area. Consequently, the fire control officer of an AC-130 aircraft switched from the low-light level television (LLLTV) to the infrared (IR) sensor. This improved the gunship's acquisition capability, but the gated laser intensifier (GLINT) tape on friendly forces was not visible in the thermal sensor. In the course of orbiting the objective, the gunner's orientation of the perimeter became confused. Without the confirmation of the GLINT tape, he acquired a friendly vehicle outside the position and reported it inside the position. In accordance with the fire support coordination measures, the gunship was cleared to engage. Mistaking the friendly fire for enemy mortar fire, the ground unit suffered several casualties before transmitting the appropriate alarm. In many ways, this incident reinforces the need for thoroughly planned and executed ROE in an urban environment to prevent fratricide.

c. Recognizing Friendly Forces. Aviation units must know the locations of friendly ground forces. In Operation JUST CAUSE, units providing fire support were informed that another unit had cleared a building to the second floor. In fact, the unit had cleared to the tenth floor and was still conducting operations in the building. Supporting units, observing fire and protruding weapons began suppressive fires. This drew return fire from the friendly unit in the building for several seconds. All units must have standardized, clearly understood procedures for marking cleared rooms, floors, and buildings in an urban area. These procedures must be practiced and discernible even in periods of limited visibility so friendly aviation units will recognize them.

8. Training Considerations

a. Background. Aviation missions cross the spectrum of operations. Even a benign environment, such as disaster relief or civilian assistance requires focused training to minimize mission risks. Baseline training requirements must address navigating on urban terrain. It must also address locating and evaluating drop zones (DZ), locating and evaluating landing zones/pickup zones (LZ/PZ), and safely negotiating manmade obstacles during a confined area takeoff, or landing.

b. Training Programs. Frequent, realistic training is required to overcome the difficulties associated with aviation urban operations. This environment requires achieving and maintaining a high degree of aircrew proficiency. The following areas should be included in unit training programs:

(1) centralized control, decentralized execution,

(2) application of ROE,

(3) low level flight and navigation,

(4) night operations,

(5) and live fire training exercises focused on target ID, terminal control, and fratricide prevention.

c. Video and simulation. These aids can enhance planning. Available sources and types of video simulation vary. Video footage may augment information regarding hazards, lighting, and human intelligence (HUMINT). The capability to "fly" a route in planning and/or rehearsal with a video or computer simulation provides advantages in mission planning and execution. Check with the military installation or urban training facility manager to determine a site's availability and capability.

Chapter II
URBAN CHARACTERISTICS

1. Background

a. Urban Characteristics. The phrases "urban terrain", "urban areas", and "built-up areas", refer to concentrations of manmade structures and associated population that alter the natural landscape. The characteristics of the urban environment are important to identify because they influence operations. Aircrew and mission planners must establish order and purpose from the apparent chaos of an urban area. These areas range from old to new, large to small, and contain populations from a few thousand to millions. Planners must make sense of this environment for successful planning.

b. Common Characteristics. Understanding the common characteristics is important to planning. These characteristics include size, patterns, population density, structural density, and building construction. One of the most significant characteristics affecting urban operations is the structural density - how close the buildings are to each other. Generally, population density is directly proportional to structural density except in cities where most of the people live in the suburbs or outskirts. When planning urban operations, the general disposition and attitude of the local population are integral to assessments regarding the population density. As experienced in Somalia, crowds can gather quickly and may interfere with operations.

2. Size

The following categories commonly are used for classifying the size of urban areas.

a. Villages. Population less than 3,000.

b. Towns and small cities (not part of a major urban complex). Population 3,000 to 100,000.

c. Large cities with associated urban sprawl. Population 100,000 to the millions. Covers hundreds of square kilometers.

d. Strip areas. Urban areas built along roads connecting towns or cities.

3. Patterns

a. Urban Patterns. Urban patterns reflect the nature of the surrounding terrain and the relationships between different areas. Classifying urban areas into patterns aids in navigation, route and LZ selection, and observation techniques. The following patterns represent the common classification patterns.

(1) Hub. The hub effect refers to an urban area's effect on maneuver. The "hub" is the central built-up area and the main city around which outlying urban areas are arrayed. The hub acts as an obstacle to surface maneuver within the sector. See Figure II-1.

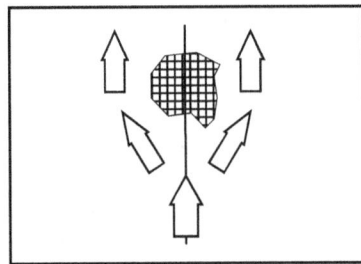

Figure II-1. Hub

(2) Satellite. It is common to find smaller, dependent built-up areas around a hub. This relationship between the primary urban area and its associated smaller towns or villages is referred to as a satellite pattern. Lines of communications (LOCs) within a satellite pattern converge on the hub. See Figure II-2.

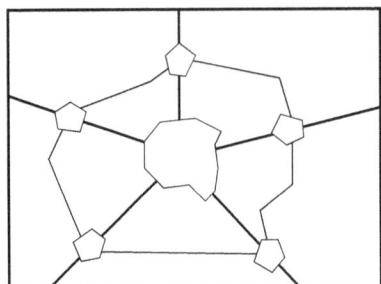

Figure II-2. Satellite

(3) Network. Network patterns are complex arrays based on the basic satellite pattern. They consist of interlocking primary hubs and subordinate satellites. LOCs within a network are more extensive than those in a simple satellite pattern and may exhibit a rectangular, rather than convergent pattern. See Figure II-3.

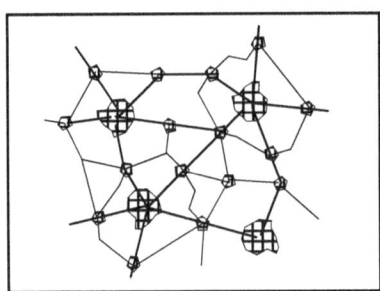

Figure II-3. Network

(4) Linear. Built-up areas often follow a linear feature or LOC. These built-up areas are commonly found along interconnecting LOCs within a satellite or network pattern. Buildings extending along major and urban strips or along the banks of a river or along a coastline are also examples of linear patterns. See Figure II-4.

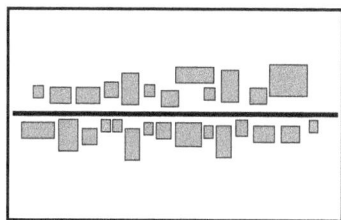

Figure II-4. Linear

(5) Segment or Pie Slice. When an urban pattern is divided by a dominant natural or manmade terrain feature, it creates a segmented pattern. Rivers, canals, major roadways, or railways can create a division of the urban area or pattern. If these features converge within the hub or urban pattern, it can create multiple segments or "pie slice" characteristics. See Figure II-5.

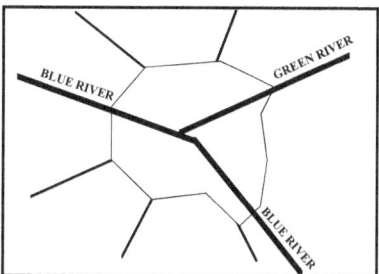

Figure II-5. Segment/Pie Slice

b. Street Patterns. Another common set of patterns in urban areas is street patterns. Streets vary in pattern and in width. Outside the US, street widths vary from 7 to 15 meters while boulevards range from 25 to 50 meters. In the US, street widths normally range from 15 to 25 meters. The following represent common street classifications.

(1) Rectangular. Streets are grid-like in pattern, with parallel streets intersected by perpendicular streets. See Figure II-6.

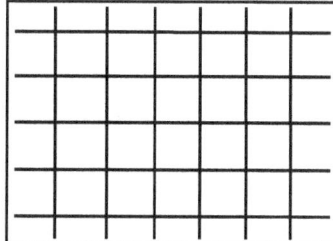

Figure II-6. Rectangular

(2) Radial. Primary thoroughfares radiate out from a central point. These streets may extend outward 360 degrees around the central point or within an arc from a point along a natural barrier, such as a coastline. See Figure II-7.

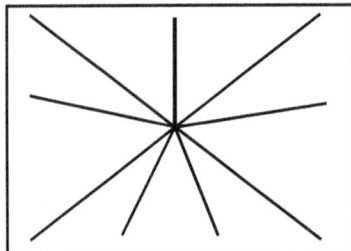

Figure II-7. Radial

(3) Concentric. A pattern of successively larger loops or rings with a common center point. This street pattern is found in conjunction with larger radial patterns. See Figure II-8.

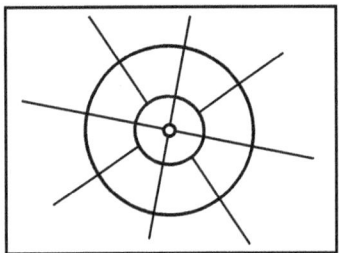

Figure II-8. Concentric

(4) Contour Conforming. Pronounced terrain relief influences construction of roadways along lines of elevation. Primary streets run parallel to the ground contour with intersecting roads connecting them. See Figure II-9.

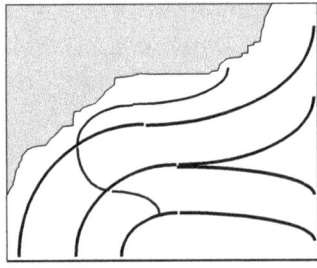

Figure II-9 Contour Conforming

(5) Irregular. Little or no discernible pattern resulting from unplanned expansion and modernization of population centers. Older European cities frequently contain an "old city" section, which characterizes this lack of pattern. See Figure II-10.

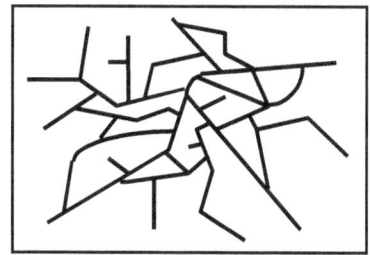

Figure II-10. Irregular

(6) Planned Irregular. Street patterns that are specifically engineered without geometric patterns for aesthetic or functional reasons. US subdivisions with curving streets and numerous cul-de-sacs are examples. See Figure II-11.

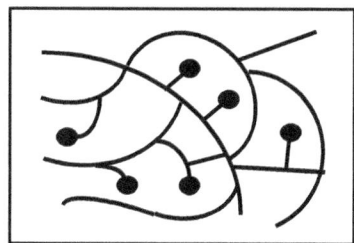

Figure II-11. Planned Irregular

4. Characteristics

a. Background. The urban patterns have characteristics affecting military operations. These characteristics can be classified as:

(1) city core,

(2) outlying high-rise,

(3) commercial ribbon,

(4) core periphery,

(5) residential sprawl,

(6) outlying industrial areas.

b. City Core and Outlying High-rise. In many cities, the core has undergone more recent development than the core periphery. As a result, the two regions are often quite different. Typical city cores consist of high-rise buildings, varying greatly in height. Modern planning for built-up areas allows for more open spaces between buildings than in old city cores or in the core peripheries. Outlying high-rise areas are dominated by this open construction style more than city cores.

c. Commercial Ribbons. These areas are characterized by rows of stores, shops, and restaurants built along both sides of major streets through built-up areas. Usually, such streets are 25 meters wide or more. The buildings are uniformly 2 to 3 stories tall, about one story taller than the dwellings on the streets behind them.

d. Core Periphery. This area consists of streets 12 to 20 meters wide with continuous fronts of brick or concrete buildings. The building heights are uniform, 2 or 3 stories in small towns, 5 to 10 stories in large cities.

e. Residential Sprawl and Outlying Industrial. These areas consist of low buildings that are 1 to 3 stories tall. Buildings are detached and arranged in irregular patterns along the streets with many open areas.

5. Population Density

a. Background. The physical characteristics of an urban area influence its population density. Population density is influenced by such urban features as roadways, public transportation, utilities, and building construction. Other factors that determine the population density include available land resources, economic resources, and cultural characteristics.

b. Land Resources. Areas with little land available for human occupation tend to be more densely populated. Geographical limitations such as mountains, waterways, or islands also tend to concentrate population.

c. Economic Resources. Economics influence population density, even with severe limitations on available land. A wealthier nation can build tall vertical structures; thus overcoming a shortage of land.

d. Cultural Characteristics. Another set of factors influencing population density is the cultural and social traits of its people. These characteristics can influence the number of civilians who choose to remain in the area, affecting the population density. If a large number of civilians leave the urban center and decrease the population density, a great concern is refugee control. If a large number of civilians remain, then the greater concern is civilian collateral damage.

6. Structural Density

a. Background. Structural density is proportional to the population density. While the following categories refer primarily to the spatial relationships between structures, the titles imply the function of an area. Building construction is assessed using these categories during the joint intelligence preparation of the battlespace (JIPB) process. See Appendix B for details. Remember that the specific type of structural density can be used for a quick direction reference, which aids situational awareness.

b. Dense, Random Construction (Type A). This type of construction is found in lesser-developed and nondeveloping nations. Close groupings of older buildings are found in the center of villages, towns, and cities. A high density of close or adjoining structures along narrow streets characterizes the oldest sections of many cities. Port-au-Prince, Haiti, with its narrow twisting roads, is good example of this construction type. A variety of construction types and materials may be present with little or no setback of structures from the street itself. In the downtown areas, buildings are often connected to each other, making ID of specific target sites extremely difficult. This construction type considerably limits LOS and fields of fire. Navigation is difficult and aircrews can become disoriented quickly without easily discernable references. See Figure II-12.

Figure II-12. Type "A"

c. Closed-Orderly Block Construction (Type B). Type B characterizes medium-size towns and large cities like Las Vegas, Nevada. These areas consist of residential and commercial buildings that often form continuous street fronts. Inner courtyards may be-contained within the block structure. See Figure II-13. Type B construction typically consists of residential and commercial buildings, small factories, and wider roads. The average street width is 26 meters allowing greater vehicle movement and possible low hover operations. This allows better fields of view and longer LOS distances. Distinct building types make identifying the objective area easier than in a dense random type of development but locating friendly forces remains difficult.

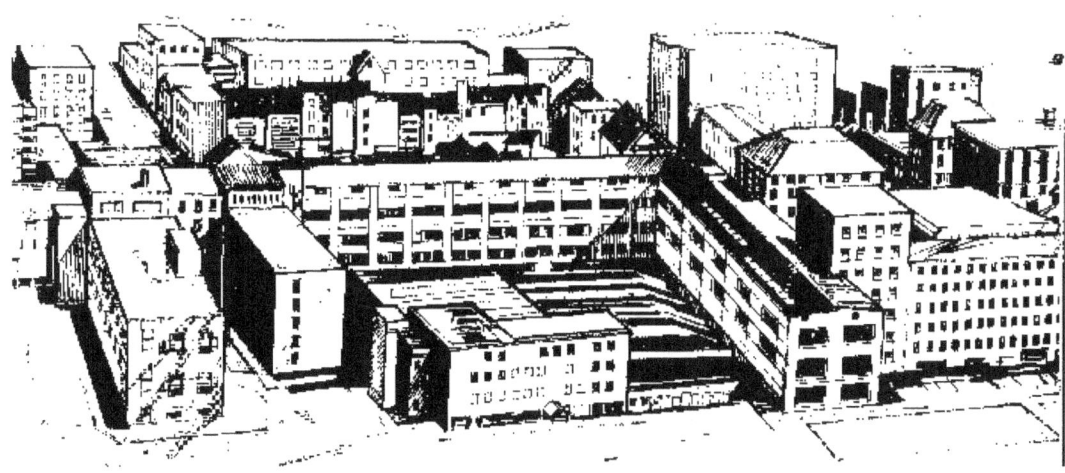

Figure II-13. Type "B"

d. Residential Area Construction (Type C). Type C areas are often contiguous to Type B areas. Residential areas are normally located on the outskirts of cities and can pose several problems for aircrews. Residential areas normally consist of rowhouses or single dwellings with yards, trees, gardens, and fences. The street widths average 14 meters, with building setback distances of 6-8 meters. This provides an effective street width or visibility corridor of up to 30 meters. Older European or colonial urban residential areas may have more narrow streets and little or no setback of the dwellings. See Figure II-14. Closely spaced houses and narrow roads may limit the availability of a suitable LZ. Suburban areas may be obstacle rich environments. Power poles, wires, and communications towers are generally numerous. Cultural lighting may affect the performance of some night vision devices (NVD). Dense concentration of buildings and civilians in these areas may significantly hamper ability to visually or electronically acquire and track ground forces. LOS communications for aviation assets should not be affected since structures tend to be limited to 1 and 2 stories.

Figure II-14. Type "C"

e. High-Rise Area Construction (Type D). Type D construction is found in medium-size and large city residential developments and business parks. High-rise cities such as Houston, Texas and Ankara, Turkey are examples. These cities contain multi-story apartment or office buildings separated by large open areas such as parking lots, parks, and individual one-story buildings. See Figure II-15. High-rise cities tend to have a stereotypical downtown area with an elevated skyline and development. These multi-storied buildings offer many challenges to the aircrew. These large, significant terrain features may simplify navigation, but tall buildings and narrow roads severely limit the ability to fly between buildings. Large open areas for LZs or DZs, such as parks and parking lots, are often adjacent to these buildings. If extremely steep ingress/approach and egress/departure angles are required for LZ/DZ access, utility may be limited. Open rooftops offer easy access to insert ground teams and extract isolated personnel, but the very nature of these multi-storied buildings may require out of ground effect hover or aircraft operating near maximum power available limitations. Depending on weather conditions, aircraft limitations may exclude this type of maneuver. The threat level coupled with the ability to gain access to rooftops and their structural integrity will influence their use. Enemy access to upper levels and rooftops may allow them to fire down on aircraft and ground forces below.

Figure II-15. Type "D"

f. Industrial/Transportation Construction (Type E). Type E areas are the most open and dispersed types. Newer industrial or transportation areas are generally located on or near the edge of towns and cities. They typically consist of low, flat-roofed factory buildings, warehouses, and railway facilities. Industrial buildings are large, functionally designed, and normally have large parking lots or work yards suitable for LZ operations. See Figure II-16. Aircraft can operate more effectively due to the low building profiles, better LOS, and reliable communications. There are some disadvantages to industrial areas. One concern is heightened exposure to secondary explosions from ordnance. Another is the flammable and explosive hazard normally found with petroleum, oil, and lubricant tanks, refineries, and factories.

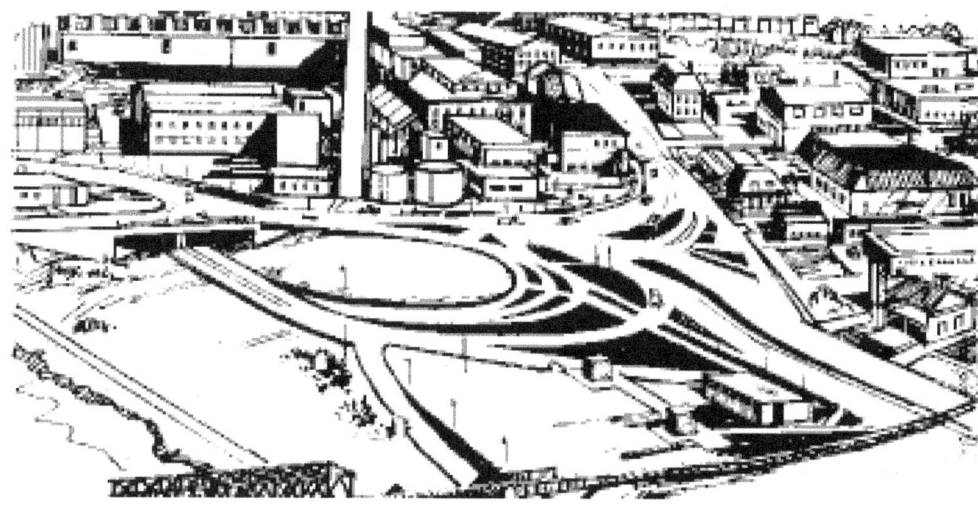

Figure II-16. Type "E"

7. Building Construction

a. Background. The construction and types of buildings within an area further define its characteristics. When looking at a city composition, planners should analyze building types, construction materials and area density. Urban areas are composed of two types of building composition, framed and mass. Knowing the difference assists in determining the effectiveness of munitions and the cover offered to personnel. In many industrialized nations with modern cities, most buildings are framed. Examples of framed buildings are the residential home with 2 x 4 (or larger) construction, numerous non load-bearing walls, and large windows. Commercial offices and high rise buildings are generally framed with steel girders. Mass buildings are built so exterior walls bear the weight of the structure. The walls of mass structures are usually thick and constructed of masonry materials such as stone, brick, or reinforced concrete. Approximately 62 percent of buildings outside the US consist of mass construction technique. Mass structures provide more protection for ground forces than framed buildings. For a more detailed discussion on the link between weapons effects and the type of building construction, reference the Joint Munitions Effectiveness Manual (JMEM).

b. Construction Types. Individual building construction is analyzed during the JIPB process. See Appendix B for more information. The definition of each type emphasizes the construction and materials of the structure. A particular single family dwelling, for example, may be more properly classified as Type 1, not Type 3 or 4. The following is a description of each type of construction:

(1) Wood and Timber Frame Construction (Type 1) (Framed Construction). Type 1 buildings have wooden rafters and weak exterior walls, offering little protection from fires. Farm buildings, older city dwellings and inexpensive private storage buildings are examples. The fire hazard for Type 1 buildings is high.

(2) Masonry Construction (Type 2) (Mass Construction). Type 2 buildings have strong stone or brick walls, and are more suitable for defense than Type 1. Older governmental or institutional buildings, such as courthouses and schools are often Type 2 construction. The fire hazard for Type 2 buildings is low.

(3) One or Two-Family Dwelling (Type 3) (Mass Construction). Type 3 buildings have walls of solid or insulating brick or cinder blocks with ceilings of reinforced concrete. They offer significant protection and require little reinforcement. Type 3 buildings often contain strongly constructed basements and are low fire hazards.

(4) Prefabricated One-Family Dwelling (Type 4) (Framed Construction). Type 4 buildings are pre-cast of light building materials and offer less protection and greater fire hazard than Type 3 buildings. These buildings frequently contain strongly constructed basements.

(5) Low-Rise Office Building (Type 5) (Framed Construction). Type 5 buildings have multi-story steel frame and reinforced concrete construction. They are frequently characterized by large expanses of glass, offering little protection from direct fire.

(6) High-rise office building (Type 6) (Framed Construction). Type 6 buildings are similar in construction and characteristics to Type 5 office buildings, but consist of six or more stories.

(7) Low-Rise Apartment Building (Type 7) (Framed Construction). Type 6 buildings are similar in size to Type 5 office buildings, but with less glass and with load-bearing reinforced concrete walls. They offer greater protection from direct fire.

(8) High-rise apartment building (Type 8) (Framed Construction). Type 8 buildings are similar in construction and characteristics to Type 7 apartment buildings, but consist of six or more stories.

(9) Industrial/Warehouse Complexes (Type 9) (Framed Construction). Type 9 building construction varies considerably, but is generally steel frame with lightweight exterior walls. Reinforced concrete floors and ceilings are found in multistory Type 9 buildings.

8. Features of Special Consideration

a. Coastal Features and Waterways.

(1) Background. All hydrography associated with urban terrain warrants careful analysis. Water features represent possible mobility obstacles to surface forces, and are a potential LOC. The presence of a coastline or major waterway is often the reason that a population center came into existence in a particular place.

(2) Port Facilities. Port facilities represent a focal point for commerce and logistics. They hold strategic significance in many cases. Control of docks and associated facilities accommodates large-scale transport functions into or out of a city. Port seizures may be a primary objective for attacking forces.

(3) Rivers and Canals. Rivers and canals can divide urban areas and represent significant physical obstacles to surface maneuver. Control of bridges and crossing sites is critical to ground mobility and security of an urban area. Major rivers are primary LOCs at a national level. Rivers can be used to transport commodities, raw materials, and finished products. Similarly, military logistics requirements can be supported by the use of rivers and canals. Aircrews should minimize exposure time over major LOCs.

b. Airfields. Airfields and other landing sites are major urban commerce and logistic centers. The flow of commercial and/or military traffic is vital to an operation. The control of these areas and the airspace around them could be a decisive factor in an operation. Airfields and improved landing areas such as wide, multi-lane, straight highways can accommodate large-scale transport aircraft. Size, load bearing capability, and aircraft parking areas figure greatly into the value of an airfield. Seizure of an airfield is often a primary objective.

c. Subterranean Features.

(1) Background. Larger cities feature a variety of subterranean systems of military significance. A complex network of tunnels and passageways may exist below the surface. While not visible or directly influencing aviation operations, subterranean features figure prominently into urban operations.

(2) Public Transport. Underground public transport systems, such as subways, represent major LOCs within the urban environment. Tunnels associated with these systems can accommodate vehicular traffic and large numbers of troops.

(3) Passageways. Some cities contain sophisticated underground pedestrian passageways and shopping "malls" in the central business district. While generally not large enough to support vehicular traffic, these complexes can be exploited for troop mobility and assembly, logistical operations, and C2. Smaller utility passageways may be quite extensive and optimal for use as infiltration routes by small forces.

(4) Waterways and Tunnels. Special operations forces (SOF), sappers, terrorists, or partisans may use underground waterways or communications tunnels. Storm sewers are generally large enough to allow troop movement. The passageways, accessed generally through manholes, may be almost as extensive as the street pattern. Sanitary sewers are usually much smaller, less accessible, and less suitable for use by troops than are storm sewers.

d. Cultural Sites. Cultural and historical sites such as churches, museums, and mausoleums, also are found routinely in urban areas. International law provides special protections for many of these landmarks. These areas may be designated in appropriate plans such as the airspace control plan. The areas may be designated as a no fly area (NFA), restricted fire area, restricted operating zone (ROZ), etc. Fire control measures for other areas such as medical treatment facilities, water purification plants, nongovernmental organization (NGO) operating locations, or other structures or areas may be designated.

Chapter III
FLIGHT OPERATIONS

1. Background

This chapter details the unique considerations of aviation urban operations. Urban operations may include combat, peacekeeping, peacemaking, and humanitarian support in non-combat environments, as well as combinations of all types. Regardless of the type of operation, detailed planning and a thorough JIPB are required. See Appendix B.

2. Threat Considerations

a. Threat Analysis. Intelligence on the threat will be difficult to obtain and more difficult to accurately update. Areas of control can change rapidly and may be confusing. Planners must anticipate rapid changes in the threat and incomplete information. Every building and structure in an urban area is a potential enemy position. The presence of snipers, vulnerability to ambush, and difficulty in distinguishing combatants from non-combatants places participants under additional psychological stress.

b. Reconnaissance. Commanders must establish reconnaissance operations early, using all available assets. Unmanned aerial vehicles (UAV) with data linked video are useful assets. Manned aircraft with multiple reconnaissance systems such as LLLTV, forward-looking infrared (FLIR), and NVDs can provide focused concentration of specific areas. These visual systems, coupled with space-based intelligence, surveillance, and reconnaissance systems (ISR) assets, electronic intelligence systems, voice interceptions, direction finding (DF) platforms networked with ground-based systems, CA, SOF, and ground forces provide a picture of the urban environment. HUMINT can provide information on threat intent and forces, as well as information about city infrastructure and status. Gathering detailed information during the planning phase of an aviation operation provides planners and aircrew with information about threat positions, movements, routes, and weapons.

c. Civilian Population. A defending enemy force normally has the advantage of familiarity with the terrain. The civilian population of the area can play an active role in the defense. Regardless of its activity, the larger the civilian population remaining within the area, the more influences it has on military operations. Enemy or friendly forces can have the support of the remaining people. Their support provides significant intelligence, logistics, and security, as well as a potential paramilitary capability.

d. Ground Threat. Urban operations often magnify the threat to aircraft. Light to medium antiaircraft artillery (AAA) may be employed from ground sites, the tops of buildings, in or near otherwise protected (attack prohibited by ROE, operational planning, etc.,) structures, or mounted on civilian vehicles, thus providing aircrews with a very complex threat picture. A man-portable air defense system

(MANPADS), with its small size, light weight, rapid engagement capability, and ease of concealment, is an excellent weapon for operating in close proximity to or on top of buildings and other structures. Heavy AAA and surface-to-air missiles (SAM) require open terrain due to radar or siting requirements. However, this does not prevent their employment within urban boundaries. The obstructions and crowded airspace of cities limit aircraft defensive maneuvering options, increasing the effectiveness of AAA, MANPADS, and SAMs while at the same time providing excellent opportunities for the establishment of ambush sites. Urban terrain provides virtually unlimited concealment, thus complicating escort missions, suppression of enemy air defenses (SEAD), and counter attack. Restricted orbits, weapons employment, and rotary-wing landing approaches increase aircraft vulnerability and limit defensive options. The terrain may also limit suppression options. The cluttered environment (e.g., lights, fires, smoke, dust, etc.) makes identification of missile launches or ground fire more difficult. Aircrews and planners should also consider the effects of fixation and visual confusion. Missions requiring landing operations must also consider ground threats such as artillery, mortars, or snipers. Planners must expand their view of what constitutes a threat to aviation operations in the urban environment.

3. Weather

a. Background. The aviation commander must establish minimum weather requirements before conducting operations. Weather conditions affect the employment of all aircraft and weapons systems. Adverse weather will hinder the employment of UAVs, radar, FLIR, laser, optical systems, NVDs, and IR weapons.

b. Ceilings. Low ceilings affect all aviation assets, especially fixed-wing aircraft. Low ceilings can obscure high rise rooftops, and other obstructions such as power lines, towers, and smokestacks. Low ceilings can also deny fixed-wing aircraft the required time and altitude to obtain a satisfactory ordnance delivery solution. The presence of high rise buildings and low ceilings decreases the effective above ground level (AGL) operating area. Low ceilings will also affect the performance of laser-guided weapons. In addition, artificial lighting against a low overcast will highlight aircraft flying under the overcast to ground observers.

c. Visibility. Smog buildup from industrial areas and vehicle exhausts also reduce visibility. Smoke from fires and dust from damage and destruction may reduce the visibility in otherwise clear conditions. Reduction in visibility can significantly degrade the performance of weapons sensors and laser or optically guided munitions.

d. Winds. In urban areas, the city structure affects wind patterns. Wind patterns are "broken up" and funneled down streets and alleys. While the wind may be calm along one end of a block, it can be turbulent at another. City structure also influences the location of turbulent areas. Therefore, predicting turbulent areas is difficult. Turbulence affects aircraft performance and weapons delivery.

e. Temperatures. IR signatures are affected by the proximity of other buildings and structures (for example, shadowing and winds). Times of thermal crossover occur when objects viewed through IR sensors may be indistinguishable due to their temperature similarities with their backgrounds. Thermal crossover in urban areas may be relatively insignificant due to shadowing effects of structures and the types of materials (e.g., asphalt, concrete, etc.) making up the background. However, when using a FLIR, aircrews must pay particular attention during this period. Furthermore, during this period, thermal crossover is particularly sensitive to wind, which can affect differences in target and background temperatures. Urban temperatures are generally higher than those in rural areas and can be 10 to 20 degrees higher than the surrounding environment. High thermal contrast can adversely affect thermal sight performance.

4. Command, Control, and Communications

a. Commander's Intent. A clear understanding of the commander's intent is an imperative for all operations, facilitating initiative in harmony with the commander's desires. Through a mission type or operation order (OPORD), the commander states his intent, allowing subordinates the initiative to achieve objectives in whatever method the subordinate deems appropriate. In the complex urban environment, maintaining communications can be difficult because of interference caused by structures restricting LOS systems. This increases reliance on decentralized execution. Detailed mission orders and briefings aid in conducting operations.

b. C3 Planning. A detailed, flexible, and redundant C3 plan is essential. Aerial or rooftop retransmission systems and the use of remote antennas may overcome some of these problems. Airborne C3 support systems (e.g., airborne battlefield command and control center (ABCCC), Airborne Warning and Control System (AWACS), joint surveillance target, attack, radar system (JSTARS), and joint airborne communications center/command post (JACC/CP) equipped C-130/C141s) may alleviate some of these difficulties. Another option is an appropriately equipped UH-60 or UH-1 helicopter. Each of these platforms has inherent capabilities and weaknesses that may make them more or less desirable for operations in urban environments. Reference system publications and joint planning publications for more detailed information on capabilities.

c. Air Asset Control. Although all air assets should remain under positive control to the greatest extent possible, procedural control measures may be required for air operations in the objective area. This is especially true in situations where airborne C3 assets are unavailable or unable to communicate due to interference. Visual signaling may also be affected by vertical development in urban areas. Normal urban clutter makes it harder to differentiate these signals from their background.

d. Common Frequency. A common frequency for all units facilitates rapid transfer and understanding of information. Specific information concerning multi-Service tactics, techniques, and procedures (MTTP) for air-to-air, air-to- surface, and surface-to-air brevity codes is found in Service manuals, Field Manual (FM) 90-38, Marine Corps Reference Publication (MCRP) 3-25B, Naval Warfare Publication (NWP) 6-02.1, and Air Force Tactics, Techniques, and Procedures (Interservice)

(AFTTP(I)) 3-2.5. The issue of common frequency use, particularly for encrypted transmission, can be greatly complicated in multinational operations. Planners should consider this issue and develop methods for in-the-clear communications if necessary.

5. Airspace Control

a. Compressed Airspace. Compressed airspace and a unique three-dimensional environment characterize aviation urban operations. These factors increase planning and execution problems, especially when in close proximity to friendly forces and non-combatants. The compressed urban airspace brings separate and diverse missions into close proximity. For example, an airdrop of supplies could be performed simultaneously with CAS missions protecting the unit being supplied. Knowledge of other missions tasked for the same area is vital to avoid interference.

b. Control Measures. Develop positive and procedural control measures for specific airspace. This will assist in eliminating mission conflicts. These measures must also consider ongoing host nation (HN) or foreign military airspace requirements. A useful method of implementing positive control is execution of a joint air tasking order (ATO) through the Theater Air Ground System (TAGS). The joint ATO assures deconfliction and synchronization of aviation assets. Multinational air assets may also be included in the joint ATO. A combination of positive and procedural control measures may be appropriate because of the potential for high volumes of air traffic over urban areas. For example, establishing a ROZ or high-density airspace control zone (HIDACZ) over the area of operations is one means to facilitate the simultaneous employment of aerial platforms. Heightened awareness of support missions operating in and throughout the general area must be maintained. Detailed information concerning multi-Service procedures for integrated combat airspace command and control (ICAC2) is provided in Service manuals, FM 100-103-1, MCRP 5-61, NWP 3-52.1, and AFTTP(I) 3-2.16.

6. Air-to-Ground Coordination

Air-to-ground coordination is improved using overlays and pictures. Figure III-1 depicts an example of a ground unit's control measures. The sketch numbers major structures and labels building corners (A-D) providing a legend to identify each building. Establishing objectives and phase lines assists in understanding the ground scheme of maneuver and is one method to integrate both air and ground operations. Specific information concerning multi-Service procedures for a TAGS is provided in Service manuals, FM 100-103-2, MCWP 3-25.2, NWP 3-56.2, and AFTTP(I) 3-2.17.

7. Maps and Charts—Selection and Preparation

a. General Considerations. Consider all types of geospatial products ranging from paper maps and charts to digital mapping databases including commercial as well as government products. Maps with a larger scale than 1:50,000 (i.e., 1:24,000 or 1:12,500) provide greater detail for urban mission planning and execution. Numerous large-scale maps exist to assist aircrews.

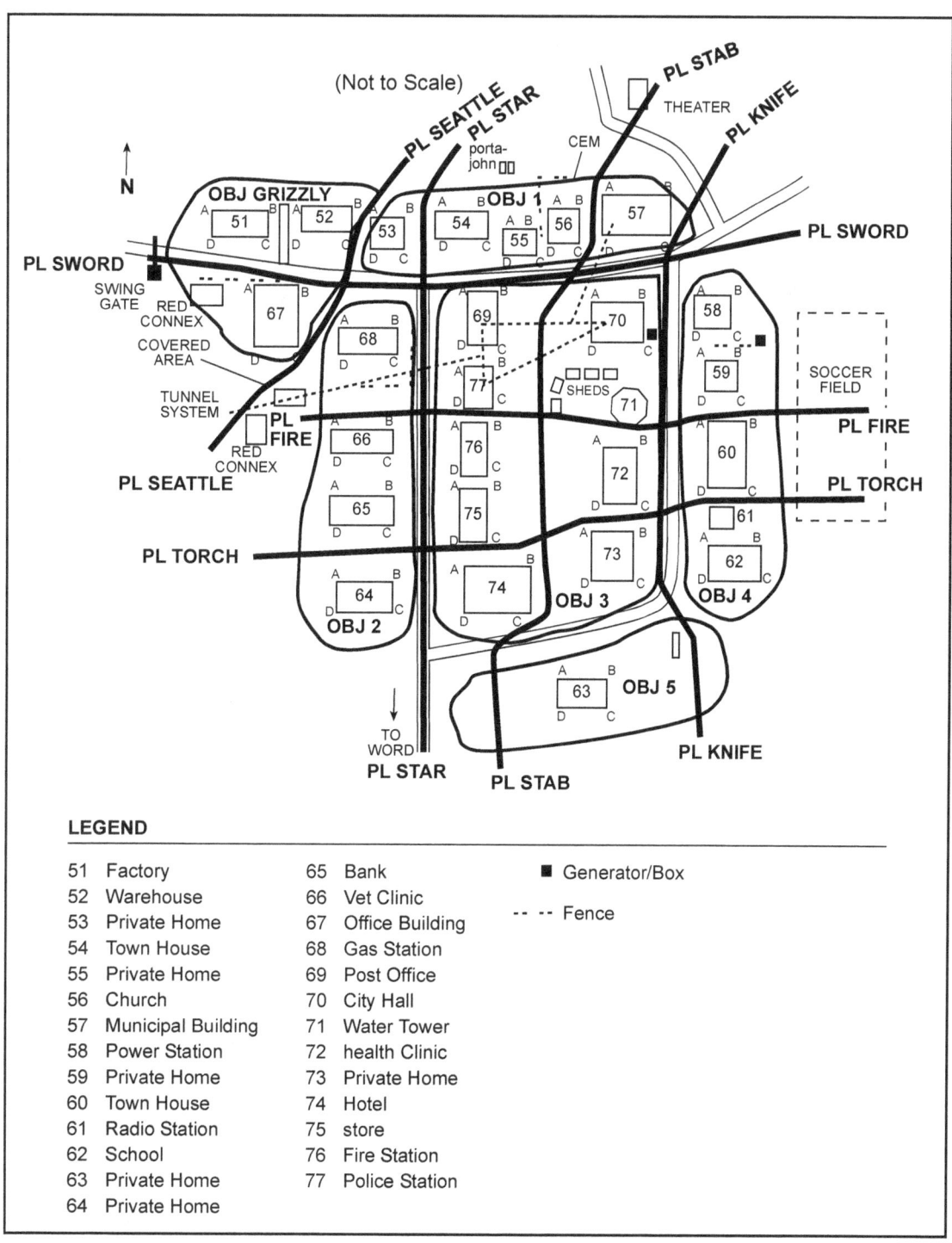

Figure III-1. Ground Unit Control Measures

LEGEND

51 Factory	65 Bank	■ Generator/Box
52 Warehouse	66 Vet Clinic	
53 Private Home	67 Office Building	-- -- Fence
54 Town House	68 Gas Station	
55 Private Home	69 Post Office	
56 Church	70 City Hall	
57 Municipal Building	71 Water Tower	
58 Power Station	72 health Clinic	
59 Private Home	73 Private Home	
60 Town House	74 Hotel	
61 Radio Station	75 store	
62 School	76 Fire Station	
63 Private Home	77 Police Station	
64 Private Home		

b. Government Products. The National Imagery and Mapping Agency (NIMA) produces 1:12,500 scale maps for specific urban areas as specified by the customer. A non-combatant evacuation operation (NEO) intelligence support handbook (NISH) is also available for every American Embassy (classified SECRET). The NISH is intended to augment the planning for NEO or hostage recovery operations and contains information such as pre-surveyed LZ listings. Planners must consider currency of terrain information during planning.

c. Civilian Maps. Commercially available civilian or tourist maps may show greater and more current urban detail than military maps. While street maps and tourist maps do not normally show terrain, they often provide useful information on current street and bridge locations, street names, shapes of prominent buildings, and cultural features. Civilian maps usually have a reference grid overlay that, if available in sufficient quantities, may be useful as a supplemental terrain reference during urban operations. However, these maps do not come marked with the Military Grid Reference System (MGRS) or universal transverse mercator (UTM) references. Although marked with a common reference grid, commercial maps or charts should not be used as a reference for employing munitions. Ensure all units disseminate any approved non-standard reference systems to enable proper target ID and fratricide prevention.

> WARNING: Check the reference system used to prepare a map or chart (i.e., World Geodetic System 1984 (WGS-84), Tokyo Special, etc.). Different datum can cause significant confusion and errors.

d. Geospatial Products. Units must maintain accurate geospatial products for their operational area and continuously update them as new features and hazards are identified. This is a shared responsibility for aircrews, intelligence personnel, and operations sections. For example, the intelligence staff, as part of the JIPB process, should conduct initial preparation of the maps and charts since intelligence sources may be the only source of hazard information before mission execution. Other sources of hazards include the airspace authority that publishes known flight hazards, such as the notice to airmen. Detailed analysis of flight hazards during mission planning is critical to safe flight operations in urban terrain. Many hazards may be unlit and difficult to discern amongst the bright ground lights. Several types of flight hazards exist:

(1) Physical Hazards. The majority of physical hazards within an urban area are manmade. These include antennas, wires, power lines, Tube-launched, optically tracked, wire-guided (TOW) missile wires, and other obstructions.

(2) Environmental Hazards. Environmental hazards include meteorological effects, extremes in artificial illumination, and unpredictable wind effects.

(3) Natural Hazards. Natural hazards include tall trees, and areas of high bird concentration.

(4) Air Traffic Hazards. The high volume of air traffic over and within urban areas is another significant hazard.

(5) Other Hazards. Other hazards include high intensity radio transmission areas. All known radio emitters should be assessed for potentially adverse effects on aircraft systems.

8. Route Planning and Navigation

a. Planning Factors. Appropriate flight profile and route selection are perhaps the most difficult planning factors. A dynamic flight profile offers the best survivability and responsiveness. Aircrews should base their flight profile on traditional factors of mission, enemy, terrain and weather, troops and support available, and time available. Special consideration must be given to the unique characteristics of urban terrain. Plan appropriate routes and altitudes to consider known threats and exploit environmental factors such as wind direction, moon angle and azimuth, and urban noise.

b. Navigation Techniques. In an urban environment, a small navigational error (i.e., a couple of city blocks) can rapidly evolve into disorientation. Although natural land features (rivers, lakes, etc.) are preferable landmarks, they may not be useable during various flight profiles. Manmade features may provide the majority of available navigation aids. If possible, pick large recognizable features for navigation. Examples include cemeteries, stadiums, cathedrals, and major roads. Linear features, such as major highways, rivers, railways, canals, and coastlines provide easily recognizable boundaries and references to assist aircrews in maintaining orientation. Prominent rail and highway interchanges are useful as en route checkpoints. However, remember that in enemy-held areas, these same prominent features might be protected by anti-air weapon systems. As aircrews become more familiar with the operational area, more use is made of local landmarks during flight.

c. Enhancing Survivability. Low-level flight techniques, adapted for urban terrain, may be employed to enhance survivability. Remaining unseen visually and electronically is the most effective method of preventing an engagement by hostile forces. Obviously, if there is no tactical reason to operate in low profiles (i.e., disaster assistance operations), higher profiles are more suitable and safer. "High" versus "low" is matter of carefully weighing the factors, making an informed decision, and remaining flexible if the situation dictates a profile change. The navigation techniques employed and the use of night systems will factor greatly into the degree of risk and effectiveness of a particular profile. Distilled to its most basic elements, the issue is this: "do aircrews want brief exposure to hostile weapons at close range, or continuous enemy observation and exposure to weapons at extended slant range?"

d. Route Planning. A network route structure of air control points (ACP) and routes (preferably surveyed) may be used to facilitate route planning, navigation and C3. See Figure III-2. ACPs are especially useful for aircraft navigation systems that require visual updates. Different sequences of ACPs appropriate to the mission may be assigned code words to facilitate operational security, control, and route changes in flight. For example, "Broadway" may be a route with ACP sequence 2, 7, and 8; "Wall Street," ACPs 1, 6, and 3; "Bourbon", ACPs 4, and 9; etc. Before ever being used in a tactical environment, a clearly defined initial point (IP) should be verified by aircrews of high performance aircraft to ensure that both IP data and aircraft systems are correct and reliable. Offset aimpoints may also facilitate target ID. The location of these points should be published in all applicable plans and

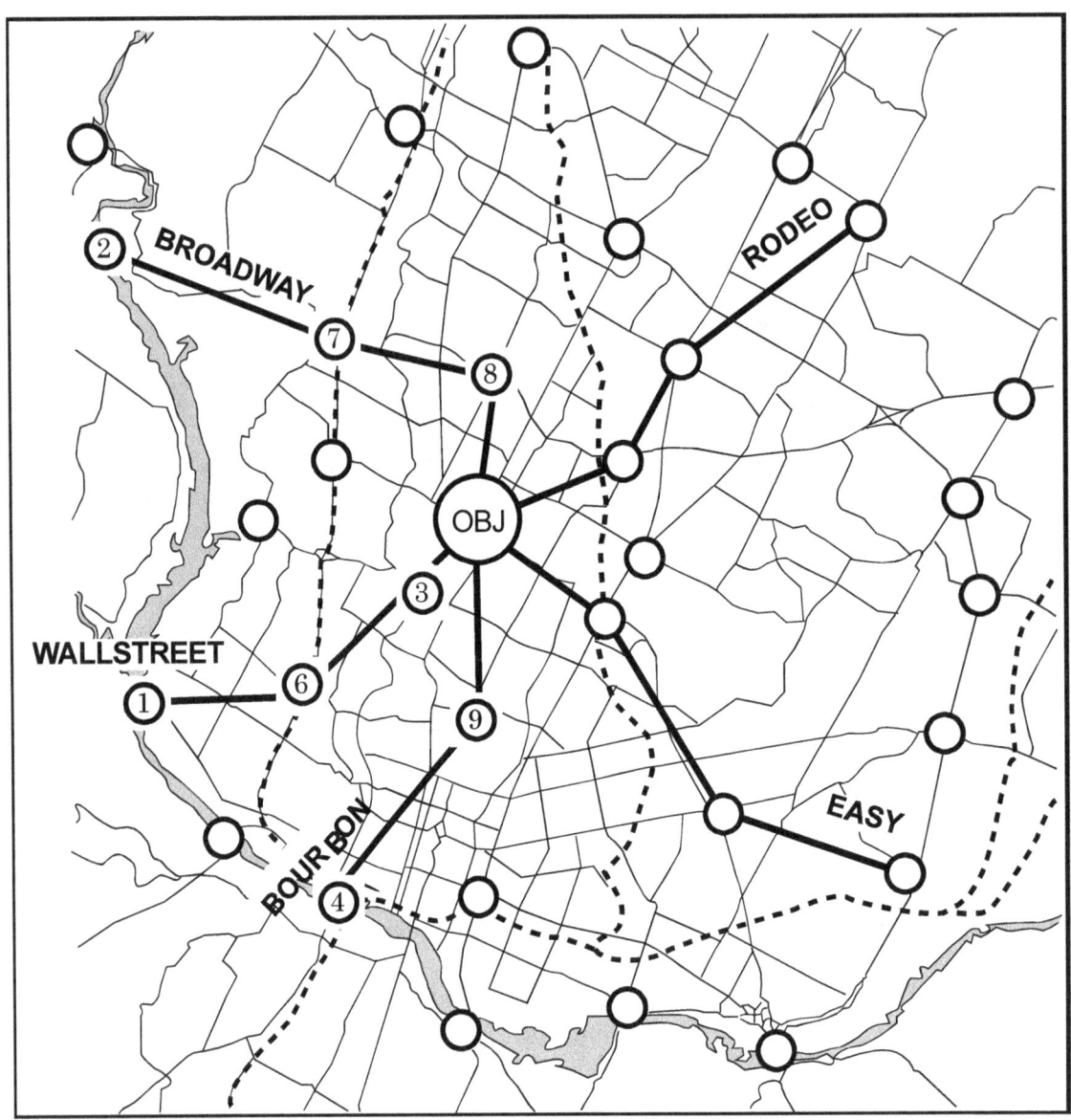

Figure III-2. Network Route Structure

orders. In situations where enemy forces are present, great care must be taken to avoid predictability of routes. Whenever possible, plan to use routes, battle positions, attack by fire positions, airspace coordination areas (ACA), holding areas, and orbits over friendly held terrain that do not expose aircraft to threats. Terrain and congested airspace may force repeated use of ACPs, LZs and flight profiles. The habitual flying of routes from one obvious feature to the next, or along LOCs, is strongly discouraged in the presence of enemy forces or potentially hostile civilians. Avoid predictability of flight routing in all but the most benign of operational environments. Track the frequency that each ACP is used to better control route over-use. Route names and "call signs" should not be re-used repetitively with the same ACP sequence. Flight profiles must take into consideration small arms, AAA, MANPAD, and SAM weapon ranges and communications.

e. Effective Navigation. Navigation over urban terrain can be more difficult than over natural terrain due to an over-abundance of cues. Navigation is also more difficult for rotary-wing aircraft because most maps do not show the vertical development of urban terrain. The high density of structures, variety of geographical references, and high light levels can create "visual saturation." Rapid displacement from position to position can sometimes create confusion between aerial and ground observers as to cardinal directions or locations. Familiarity with the characteristics of urban terrain allows aircrews to discern key features in this environment. Navigational aids, such as the global positioning system (GPS), have reduced but not eliminated this problem. Effective navigation over large towns and cities can require the use of a variety of navigational systems and techniques. The use of GPS eases the problems associated with night navigation and orientation; whereas, handheld laser pointers or designators ease the problems associated with orientation and target ID. Aircrews must monitor their equipment closely and crosscheck their position by all available means. Navigation systems may be degraded due to interference induced by buildings. Aircrews should perform detailed mission planning to maximize the effectiveness of all available assets.

9. Night Vision Devices

a. Considerations. When planning for and employing NVDs, aircrews must pay careful attention to the color, location, and intensity of urban lights, in addition to the moon angle and lunar illumination along the flight route and in the objective area. Night imagery of the area is an important tool for effective analysis and mission planning. To determine when and where to use NVD, image intensifiers, or IR sensors, a detailed analysis of the area is necessary. Aircrews should prepare to make frequent and rapid transitions from aided to unaided flight during urban flights.

b. Characteristics. Night vision goggles (NVG), and FLIR/Integrated Display System (IDS) are affected by the composition and surface conditions of urban terrain. A rural battlefield has a somewhat homogeneous composition where man-made objects contrast sharply. However, in an environment that consists primarily of manmade objects there is very little consistency in the thermal/visual scene. High light levels in urban areas create special problems. The volume and irregular patterns of ground lights in urban areas affect NVG operations. The FLIR/IDS is an excellent identification aid for terrain features and hazards in brightly-lighted night urban environments as it is not susceptible to blooming effects from overt lighting as are NVG. Brightly lit cities can be navigated without NVDs, but discerning detail in darkened areas or shadows requires using image intensifiers or IR sensors. Relatively dark areas, such as large city parks, are readily identified and make good navigation references at night. Cultural lighting will often washout NVG, decreasing their effectiveness.

c. Environmental Concerns.

(1) Lighting Condition. Operations conducted during twilight, dawn, or dusk may present problems. The rapid changes in the illumination during these periods and the inability of the eyes to quickly adjust make it difficult for aircrews to

observe terrain features and see other aircraft. FLIR devices are not affected by artificial light and are generally effective navigation and targeting systems during this period. However, they are subject to being overpowered by intense heat sources within their field of view. Very hot areas, such as factory smoke stacks or fires, make the details of objects with lower thermal contrast difficult to discern. Hostile forces may attempt to degrade the effectiveness of thermal systems by lighting bonfires, buildings, cars, tires, etc. in the area of operations. If a supported ground unit is using laser pointers, aircrews using FLIR will not be able to detect the spot. The laser pointer is detectable with NVG.

(2) Thermal Clutter. FLIR/IDS thermal clutter occurs when there are a number of objects in the sensor's field of view with approximately the same thermal signature. These objects can be "cool", leading to an overall dark image, or "hot" enough to result in an image saturated with bright spots. Overlapping hot spots results in overall reduced image quality. Using the gain and/or polarity functions can enhance FLIR/IDS imagery enough to highlight cultural features. Smoke from a smoke grenade and/or burning diesel fuel will not affect the FLIR/IDSs performance. A good rule of thumb is that if you can detect a target with a FLIR/IDS and consistently employ the laser ranging and designation functions, then you can most likely designate and lase the target satisfactorily for a laser-guided weapon. Generally all buildings will be seen and recognizable on the FLIR/IDS. Building roofs will present a different signature from walls due to the material emissivity, and this may act as another cue aiding target acquisition. If aircraft are forced to operate below 200' AGL, then the low slant angle will make building acquisition difficult and personnel/vehicle target acquisition more difficult. Slight variations in construction material for either roads or structures can alter the image enough to inhibit target acquisition and tracking. For example, while the terminal guidance controller may see an NVG image of two contrasting materials around a target, the aircrews using a FLIR/IDS may not see the same contrast due to the differences in temperature and emissivity. Furthermore, airspeed and altitude can have the same affect.

(3) Thermal Reflection. Thermal reflections can produce odd signatures, making target ID difficult. Smooth or glassy surfaces such as windshields, unpainted metal surfaces, or water are examples of thermal reflectors. They can reflect IR radiation images, like a mirror, of other nearby sources. They can appear very dark because they reflect the low radiant temperatures from the night sky. Most buildings constructed from concrete or brick will have high thermal mass, meaning their rate of temperature gain will be slow during the day (until noontime) and rate of loss will be slow during the night. Urban structures viewed mid-day can be distinctly different from a late afternoon view after having been heated throughout the day; structures of plywood or aluminum lose heat quickly and provide high thermal contrast with backgrounds that cool more slowly. As late afternoon approaches, heat dissipates quickly. In the morning, objects facing the sunrise will heat more quickly, appearing hotter than objects that face away from sunrise. Air conditioning or heating units on buildings can produce localized hot spots. Windows will appear very dark when reflecting the night sky temperature. However in a combat zone, as was seen in Bosnia, many building windows may be broken out.

(4) Smoke/Fog. FLIR/IDS visibility through fog or smoke is very good. However, smoke from burning phosphorous or flares significantly hinder thermal transmission. The atmosphere can attenuate transmission of IR energy through refraction, absorption or scattering. High water vapor concentrations, which occur at high humidity, are responsible for the majority of IR absorption. Urban areas can have significant concentrations of carbon dioxide, which is also an IR absorber, can potentially degrade FLIR/IDS performance. In practice, carbon dioxide absorption does not usually impact FLIR performance.

10. Rotary-Wing Operations

a. Background. A typical rotary-wing urban flight profile consists of modified low-level and contour techniques. Aircrews must evaluate obstacles, ambient light levels, and available navigation cues as well as types and locations of threat sources to determine the optimum altitude and airspeed. Maintaining higher airspeeds can minimize exposure time. To limit exposure to antiaircraft weapons, the preferred method of ingress and egress is a low, swift flight profile. However, slower flight speeds may be necessary to allow enough time to precisely identify and navigate to the objective area. Avoid true nap-of-the-earth flight as it exposes the aircraft to a greater potential for engagements. Slow speeds coupled with low altitudes can put the aircraft and aircrews at greater ground threat risk (small arms, rocket-propelled grenades, etc.). A low density of structures or extensive enemy use of high rooftops diminishes the masking advantages of low flight profiles. To buffer obstacle and hazard clearance, a higher flight altitude (300 to 500 feet AGL) over a city, day or night may be necessary. However, flight at higher en route altitudes exposes the aircraft to observation as it approaches the objective and makes it far more vulnerable to engagement during the descent for landing. This exposes aircraft to shoulder-launched or radar-guided SAM threats. However, the trade-off provides a better margin of safety from the hazards of unlit towers, cranes, and power-lines that blend into the urban landscape and are more difficult to detect.

b. Flight Profile. Areas of consideration when determining flight profiles include:

(1) The mission requirements.

(2) The hazards to flight.

(3) The integrated air defense system (IADS) in use by adversary forces.

(4) The small arms threat.

(5) The terrain relief and building height in and around the area.

(6) The density of structures.

(7) The accessibility/security of high, dominant rooftops.

(8) The dominant natural terrain around the urban area.

(9) The SAM threat.

c. Multi-ship Operations. Multi-ship rotary-wing operations are challenging and can require application of unique formation techniques, especially when operating with NVDs. To prevent the loss of visual contact with other aircraft among ground lights, a non-traditional vertical "stack-down" formation positioning may be required. Planning must include formation break-up and rendezvous procedures if visual contact is lost within the flight or evasive maneuvering is executed. When multiple aircraft are operating together, consider greater formation spacing to facilitate more flexible maneuvering while still providing mutual support. A wingman flying in a vertical "stack down" position from the preceding helicopter will not have the flexibility of maneuver normally enjoyed in the traditional vertical "stack up" position. Maintain a position that compensates for the illumination pollution, but avoids jeopardizing the aircraft by greater exposure to obstacle hazards or increased formation collision potential.

> WARNING: If stacking down, pay strict attention to disk spacing and have a pre-briefed formation break-up plan. Formation break-up from a stack-low position is more dangerous than from a stack-high position.

d. Aircraft Lighting. For both day and night operations, Aircrew should experiment with aircraft external lighting to best accommodate the mission, otherwise follow standing operating procedures (SOP). If overt external lighting is mandated, use the flash position to better distinguish aircraft from static light sources. In brightly-lighted areas, covert lights may not be visible. Aircrew should weigh mission lighting needs against the possibility of visual detection by the enemy. During Operation JUST CAUSE, reflective tape was placed on all friendly aircraft to assist in identification during ingress and egress. Bright ambient illumination can be favorable at times. During Operation EASTERN EXIT, the 1991 NEO operations in Somalia, evacuees commented that in the darkened landing zone, they could hear the helicopters but did not see them until they were already on the ground.

11. Fixed-Wing Operations

a. AC-130 Gunship Operations. Due to AC-130 characteristics and their requirement to fly under the protection of darkness in higher threat environments, special consideration must be given to the threat. Commanders and planners must consider the threat determined in the JIPB process before tasking the AC-130 because its effectiveness in interdiction or ground support missions could be limited by a number of factors unique to the urban environment. Using a wide range of altitude and orbit patterns, the AC-130 is a versatile platform and can perform missions ranging from C3 to CAS. If employed correctly, the AC-130 can provide commanders with excellent situational awareness. The AC-130H and the AC-130U currently employed generally operate in the same manner but have some differences. The AC-130U is all weather capable for interdiction and can predict impact points of fired ordnance. Reconnaissance in instrument meteorological conditions is degraded due to the ability to detect only radar significant targets (i.e., buildings, LOCs, vehicles, etc.), but not enemy personnel. In visual meteorological conditions, both the "H" model and the "U" model are effective. While in the weather, use of radar beacons along with a target reference points (TRP), grid, UTM, or latitude/longitude are highly desirable to identify friendly positions and initiate calls for fire. During night operations, the AC-130 can provide excellent covert illumination with its IR spotlight.

b. Fighter/Attack Operations (AV-8, A-10, F-16, F/A-18, etc.). Missions involving these aircraft take into consideration en route threat status, weather, and airspace restrictions in much the same manner as missions in non-urban environments. If friendly ground forces or non-combatants are a factor, aircrews will conduct the mission as a CAS mission. If friendly ground forces or non-combatants are not a factor, then it may be conducted as a strike mission. For example, this method was used during operations in Kosovo and Serbia in 1999. Once in the target area, terminal procedures are governed by target area threats, location of friendly forces or civilians, onboard sensor and weapon availability, and specific target geometry. For example, in a low threat environment status, aircraft can orbit the objective overhead for target acquisition in support of the ground element. As the threat level increases, aircrew may elect to offset from the threat while keeping sensors on the target area. They may also choose to climb or employ contact point to IP ingress tactics.

c. Airlift Operations. Airlift missions, in general, can be broadly categorized as either airland or airdrop. By far, the vast majority of airlift missions are airland. Consequently, since most airfields are in or near cities, most airlift missions will involve some planning for urban environments. Airdrop missions may be conducted in conjunction with humanitarian and disaster-relief efforts and often will be performed in or near urban environments. Direct airdrop support of ground forces operating in urban areas, while relatively rare, will require precise navigation and considerable pre-mission planning/coordination. In the event of humanitarian or disaster-relief missions, aircrews and planners may be required to coordinate with numerous NGO relief agencies, many of which are unfamiliar with airlift and military operations. Prior coordination and direct control of these personnel during drop and on/off load operations will greatly aid in safe mission performance.

(1) En Route Operations. Basic planning considerations for en route portions of both airland and airdrop missions in urban areas should be the same as for operations in other environments. The nature of urban terrain, however, can limit the flexibility of how these considerations are applied. For instance, formation airdrop operations increase mass on target and shorten the time required to secure drop zones. Urban areas, however, may not allow the use of large formations due to confined airspace, obstacle altitudes, and the requirement for verbally initiated release system (VIRS) drops. These limitations drive planners to the use of multiple small formations or single ship operations. Likewise, the nature of urban threats and the inability to positively secure airfields 24 hours a day can severely limit route and altitude selection for airland missions. Humanitarian and disaster-relief missions, as well as normal logistics support missions, can involve considerable threat to aircrews due to political sensitivities and the possibility of terrorist activities. The capability to use aircraft defensive systems over or near urban areas

for either airland or airdrop missions, particularly if those missions are considered "non-combat" in nature, may need to be coordinated in advance.

(2) Airland. Approach and departure operations at urban airfields where threats have been identified or are suspected cause planners significant problems. Aircraft are most vulnerable during approach and departure due to their slow speed, configuration, predictability, and lack of maneuverability. Close proximity of buildings and LOCs to flight paths will require either the use of security measures (e.g., helicopter or foot patrols of the area at random intervals) or specific aircraft tactics (e.g., random steep or shallow approaches/departures) to lessen the possibility of attack. These efforts will be less effective if structural density increases near the airfield. Tactical approach selection must be based on threat, terrain, obstacles, and the proximity of the airfield to significant urban features not under the control of security forces. The use of overt aircraft external lighting should be carefully considered when MANPADS threats are a possibility. Coordination with air traffic control (ATC) and airfield defense forces is mandatory to ensure safety and prevent fratricide. This may involve considerable coordination with HN personnel. Aircrews should be aware that control of civilians on runways has been a problem in past humanitarian operations. Vigilance during approaches to minimally controlled airfields in urban areas must be practiced to ensure go-arounds can be performed in the event civilians cross or enter runway areas.

(3) Airdrop. As with all airdrops, primary considerations for urban airdrop missions will revolve around drop and escape procedures, locations and markings of DZs, run-ins, IP selection, and aircraft/formation tactics. The unique aspects of urban terrain and their effects on airdrop missions must be considered to ensure success. The large numbers of visual cues found in urban terrain (e.g., buildings, lights, vehicles, etc.) will complicate DZ marking and route visual turn point ID. Positive radio contact with DZ personnel may be more difficult and take longer to establish due to interference from structures/electronic sources. The possibility of unapproved personnel on the DZ must be considered and additional no-drop procedures should be coordinated. Be aware that DZ control personnel may offset from the proposed DZ area to avoid giving away its position and, consequently, enable civilians to "rush" the airdrop loads.

12. Airfields

a. Background. Many airfields are located in or near urban areas. Planning for aviation urban operations should include an assessment of available airfield facilities. Urban airfield operations are a challenge for forces tasked with operating and securing them. The airfield location is known and easily identified. Aircraft may be vulnerable during approach, landing, hover, and departure operations even to low technology threat systems.

b. Airfield Operations. On the ground, aircraft are susceptible to surface-to-surface threats such as artillery, mines, booby traps, mortars, rockets, missiles, and weapons of mass destruction. Planners should also anticipate and include in their assessment the presence of major roads and the proximity of urban structures and industrial facilities in and around the airfield approach/departure routes. As a minimum, consider the following when planning airfield operations:

(1) Arrival and departure routing and maneuver limitations,

(2) Size of useable runways (length/width/obstructions),

(3) Turnaround areas and the capability for emergency departure,

(4) Taxiways and obstructions to taxi routes,

(5) Aircraft and vehicle parking areas, on/offload sites, access to each,

(6) Ground access routes and securing them,

(7) Security of airfield buildings and the perimeter,

(8) Hazardous terrain, towers, buildings, wires, etc. near flight areas,

(9) Instrument/visual procedures,

(10) Terminal area threats,

(11) Weather,

(12) Base infrastructure and billeting for aerial port of debarkation personnel,

(13) Security of approach and departure corridors,

(14) Fuel and fuel transfer support.

13. Helicopter Landing Zones (HLZ)

a. Background. Studying city composition, imagery, and maps provides a good foundation for choosing HLZs. Updated imagery should be reviewed to accurately assess HLZ size and hazards. If possible, imagery should be taken at the same time of day that the HLZs are to be used. This allows analysis of illumination and shadow conditions to be encountered during the actual mission. Ground photos can provide valuable hazard information and terrain reference. Carefully examine HLZ/PZ reports and diagrams from reconnaissance assets and make these available to all participants. Annotate all images and diagrams with magnetic north and navigation references.

b. Selection. Consider selecting an urban HLZ that is readily identifiable and accessible. Most major cities have urban parks near the central business district that may provide a suitable HLZ. Other potential HLZs include athletic stadiums, parking lots, and rooftops. Alternate HLZs in the objective area and emergency HLZs en route should be planned to the same degree of detail as primary HLZ. Some structures can accommodate helicopters landing on the rooftop. In cases where the load bearing capacity can be readily evaluated, (such as with existing rooftop helipads or with the availability of building design data), rooftops constitute viable HLZs. Some major cities have codes requiring rooftop helipads for buildings taller than a certain number of stories. These pads may have the maximum weight bearing capacity painted on the pad. The load bearing capacity of a rooftop cannot be accurately determined by simple observation. Roof clutter, such as antennas, lightning rods, and wires, can obstruct the landing area. Aircrews must also be aware of the unpredictable wind and venturi effects associated with flight in close proximity to very tall buildings, as well as out-of-ground-effect operating requirements. These effects can require additional power during operations to and from high rise rooftops.

c. Quality. HLZs, particularly those suitable for large multi-ship formations, are often limited in urban terrain. A careful balance must be made between the limited availability of suitable HLZs and exposure to observation, direct fire, or an ambush. Consider whether the mission is conducted during daylight or darkness. Daylight allows rapid ingress, egress, and facilitates navigation, but also allows for easier observation and engagement by the enemy. Night or NVG missions offer improved concealment and HLZ security, but require slower airspeeds and increase the difficulty of navigation.

d. Tactical Considerations. The tactical considerations for HLZ/PZ selection, including mission, location, and security, are exacerbated in urban terrain. If there are more aircraft than a single HLZ can accommodate, select multiple HLZs in proximity to the objective. Control measures must be adequate to deconflict the movement of all elements. Formations of assault helicopters should be no larger than will be able to land at the HLZ simultaneously. All secondary or alternate HLZs should be at least the same size to prevent unnecessary exposure to aircraft waiting to land. Give special consideration to the possibility that threats from multistory buildings can be above the vertical fields of fire of the aircraft gunners.

e. Alternate Insertion/Extraction (AIE). Aircrews can use a variety of techniques for AIEs onto rooftops. These methods include:

(1) remaining light on the landing gear after touchdown,

(2) hovering with a single skid or landing gear touching the structure,

(3) rappelling,

(4) fast rope,

(5) rope ladders,

(6) hoist operations.

If rooftop insertions are attempted, planners must consider enemy line of sight to the rooftop and potential exposure of helicopters and troops to enemy fire while in critical flight profiles. If more than one insertion/extraction element is required, consider utilizing multiple insertion flight profiles to remain unpredictable and to avoid objective area congestion. In general, fast ropes and hoist cables are manufactured in fixed lengths. Planners must ensure that AIE equipment requirements and availability are determined and that missions are not assigned that exceed current inventories and configurations.

14. Special Use Areas

a. Drop Zone. The availability of usable DZs may be limited. Parks, roads, railroad yards, airfields, athletic stadiums, and industrial storage sites are the most likely locations for airdrops. DZ operations in urban terrain are difficult due to surface obstructions, navigation, and positive ID of the DZ. Communications limitations, positive marking, DZ control, and the availability of accurate, timely intelligence also affect airdrop accuracy. Lessons learned from recent operations emphasize the importance of positively controlling personnel near the DZ, or concealing DZ locations until immediately before airdrops occur. This reduces the possibility of situations where civilians are injured by the airdrop. One exception to this is the airdrop of meals ready to eat (MRE), which have been conducted directly over urban areas using the tri-wall aerial distribution system that free-falls and spreads individual packets over a wide area.

b. Forward Arming and Refueling Point (FARP). Assessment of potential FARP locations is similar to the basic considerations for LZ/PZ selection. Consider the location's ability to accommodate the refueling/rearming element, the number of points required, whether the landing and holding area is adequately sized for the number and type of aircraft to be used, and if there is sufficient movement area. Aircraft in an urban FARP are vulnerable during refuel/rearm operations due to the proximity of concealment for threat forces. FARP locations should provide concealment from the surrounding terrain, buildings, and facilitate securing potential ground entry and exit routes. Sports stadiums may be suitable for this purpose.

c. Contingency Areas. Loitering in-flight over urban terrain is very dangerous, especially during day combat operations. Planning for in-flight contingencies may require use of assembly areas (AA) or holding areas. When necessary, plan to loiter or hold at control points well away from the urban area. The selection of AAs or holding areas requires the same consideration of technical and tactical factors as HLZs and FARPs. Selection of the proposed area(s) requires a security assessment. Concealment, the presence of friendly ground forces for security, and protective or covered facilities for personnel and equipment also must be considered. The communications plan must ensure an adequate communications capability with elements in the holding area. This can involve the use of an airborne command and control asset or retransmission platform.

Chapter IV
WEAPONS EMPLOYMENT

> *"We cannot destroy or significantly damage the infrastructure of a foreign urban center in pursuit of mission attainment and expect the population to remain friendly to either US forces or those we support. Neither can we indiscriminately use force in imprecise ways that cause unnecessary non-combatant casualties."*
> The Defense Science Board Report on MOUT

1. Introduction

Aviation urban operations require extensive intelligence collection and a flexible and capable targeting capability. Weapons requirements for urban operations can be different from those for open terrain operations. Planners must consider military necessity, proportionality, collateral damage, non-combatant casualties, and precision engagement weapons. The ordnance requirements for a specific mission must focus on the target, employment techniques, minimum collateral damage, and the capability to safely employ in proximity to friendly ground forces.

2. Weapons Selection

a. Background. The focus of weapons selection is to produce a desired weapons effect on a target while avoiding fratricide and minimizing collateral damage. Other factors influencing weapons selection are commander's intent, LOW/LOAC, ROE, day or night employment, target type, proximity of buildings, and friendly/non-combatant positions. In the urban environment, some type of precision munitions is often the first choice. Non-precision munitions may be used depending on the situation.

b. Collateral Damage. Minimizing collateral damage protects non-combatants and property, facilitates future operations, and reduces the costs of rebuilding. The presence and proximity of friendly ground forces and the effects of rubble can be essential considerations in weapons selection. To achieve the desired level of damage, it is necessary to carefully select the weapons load (Appendix C). For example, cluster and general purpose munitions are effective against troops and vehicles in the open. On the other hand, hardened, mobile, or pinpoint targets may require precision munitions. In all cases, the requesting commander should know the type of munitions scheduled for delivery, and the residual effects caused by these munitions (e.g., unexploded ordnance).

c. Considerations. Planners and aircrew must consider the following when choosing weapons.

(1) Hard, smooth, flat surfaces with 90-degree angles are characteristic of man-made targets. Due to aviation delivery parameters, munitions will normally

strike a target at an angle less than 90 degrees. This can reduce the effect of munitions and increase the chance of ricochets. The tendency of rounds to strike glancing blows against hard surfaces means that up to 25 percent of impact-fuzed rounds do not detonate when fired onto rubbled areas.

(2) Engagement times are short. Enemy personnel can present fleeting targets of opportunity; thus, the actual amount of time from target discovery to identification as hostile to weapons application can be very limited.

(3) Depression and elevation limits create dead space. Tall buildings form deep canyons that are often safe from indirect fire. Target engagement from oblique angles, both horizontal and vertical, must be considered.

(4) Smoke, dust, and shadows mask targets. Additionally, rubble and man-made structures can mask fires. Targets, even those at close range, tend to be indistinct.

(5) Urban fighting often involves units attacking on converging routes. The risks from friendly fires, ricochets, and fratricide must be considered during the planning of operations. During operations, control measures must be continually adjusted to reduce risks. Ground units must clearly mark their positions to avoid fratricide.

(6) Friendly and enemy ground forces might be inside, outside, or around the same building. The surrounding environment in urban operations means that the effect of the weapon and the position of friendly/enemy personnel with relation to structures must be considered. Usually the man-made structure must be attacked before enemy personnel inside can be attacked. Therefore, choose weapons and demolitions for employment based on their effects against the buildings material composition rather than against enemy personnel.

(7) Munitions can produce secondary effects, such as fires.

3. Tactical Target Development

> **NOTE**: The urban environment presents a variety of potential targets. In addition to military target types, staffs and aircrews must train to effectively analyze all potential targets, determine if they are suitable for engagement, and select the type and quantity of weapons required to achieve the desired results.

a. This section focuses on urban target development. For specific guidance on targeting, planners should refer to FM 6-20-10/MCRP 3-1.6.14, Tactics, Techniques, and Procedures for the Targeting Process. Criticality, accessibility, recoverability, vulnerability, effect, and recognizability (CARVER) is one method that may be used by tactical targeting planners to analyze urban tactical targeting.

(1) Criticality. A target is critical when its damage or destruction has significant influence on the enemy's ability to conduct or support operations. Consider each target in relative importance to other targets of the same complex designated for attack. The criticality of a target is dependant on the situation. For example, when an enemy has few locomotives, railroad bridges may be less critical as targets; however, safeguarding bridges may be critical when friendly forces require using them later.

(2) Accessibility. A target is accessible when it can be occupied physically or covered by direct or indirect weapons fire.

(3) Recoverability. Target recoverability is measured in time; i.e., how long it takes the enemy to replace, repair, or bypass the destruction/damage inflicted on the target.

(4) Vulnerability. A target is vulnerable if a force has the means to attack it.

(5) Effect. The possible military, political, economic, and/or sociological impacts of target attack, for example, enemy reprisals against local civilians, must be considered.

(6) Recognizability. A target or target component is recognizable if it can be identified under varying weather, light, and seasonal conditions without confusion with other targets or components.

b. Tactical aviation operations involve targeting structures, vehicles, roads, personnel, and underground objects dispersed in the urban infrastructure. Refer to the JMEM for appropriate weapons recommendations to achieve desired results.

(1) Structures. Structures can be grouped into those that may or may not be destroyed. Situations will occur where both friendly and enemy troops are in the same building. Eliminating the enemy without causing harm to friendly troops can be achieved with careful weapons selection and placement.

(2) Vehicles. Vehicles are another element of consideration in an urban environment. Confined spaces and unpredictable routes make targeting moving vehicles difficult. Since urban operations inherently generate close quarters engagements, an aircraft simply may not have time to achieve a firing solution on a moving vehicle. Passing a fire mission request to an aircraft as early as possible is a necessity.

(3) Roads and bridges. These restricted avenues of movement can work in favor of the friendly forces. Air assets can destroy, or make impassible, roads or bridges to impede the enemy's progress. A destroyed roadway can isolate an enemy unit or force them to abandon their vehicles, both of which could be to the benefit of the friendly ground forces. However, once an obstacle is created, it becomes an obstacle to both sides.

(4) Personnel. Engaging personnel in urban terrain is difficult due to the abundance of cover. If limiting collateral damage is also a consideration, the problem is compounded. Ground force assistance in tracking and target ID is critical. Aircrews will have to select appropriate weapons to get the desired results.

(5) Underground. Underground targets, such as basements, subways, and bunkers, require careful weapon consideration. Although many of the types of weapons used in urban CAS do not have the ability to penetrate underground targets, damaging their access could be the only results required. Ground forces identifying entrances and exits to underground sites will allow air assets to destroy these and effectively remove them as a potential threat to ground forces or as a useable sanctuary for enemy forces.

4. Targeting Grids and Reference Techniques

Ground maneuver elements generally use a terrain-based reference system during urban operations. MGRS coordinates have little meaning at street level. Common control methods include urban grid (Figure IV-1), bullseye targeting (Figure IV-2), objective area reference grid (Figure IV-3), and TRPs (Figure IV-4). These techniques are based on the street and structure pattern present, without regard to the MGRS grid pattern. Aircrew must plan to transition to the system in use by the ground element upon arrival in the objective area. For example, references to the objective or target may include local landmarks such as, "The third floor of the Hotel Caviar, south-east corner." This transition should be facilitated by using a "big to small" acquisition technique.

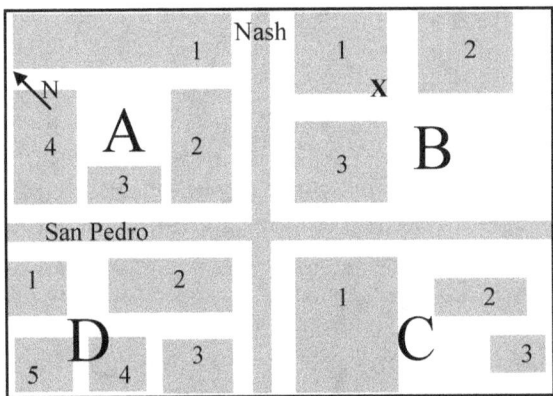

Bravo-1, south corner. Sniper top floor window."

Figure IV-1. Urban Grid

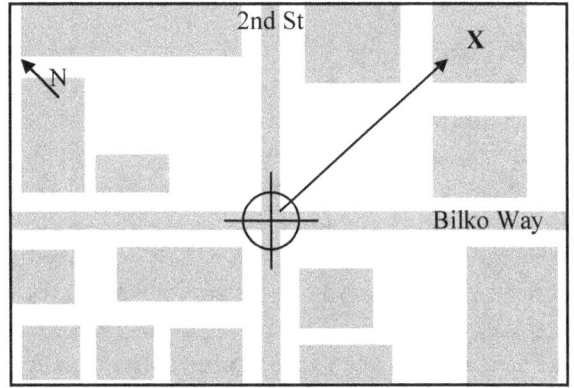

Figure IV-2. Bullseye Targeting

"Bullseye, Charlie. 105 degrees magnetic, 250 meters, ZPU on the roof."

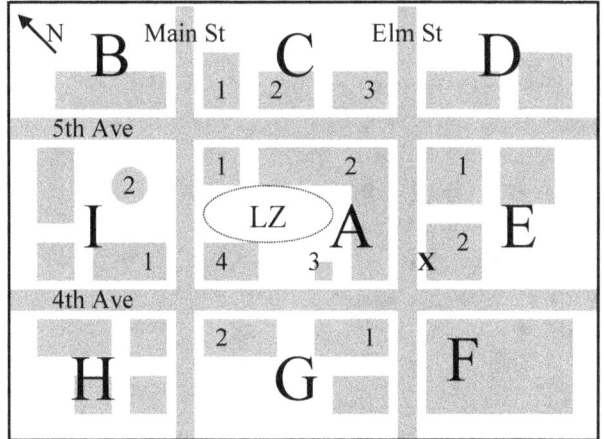

Figure IV-3. Objective Area Reference Grid

"Echo-2, main entry on Elm."

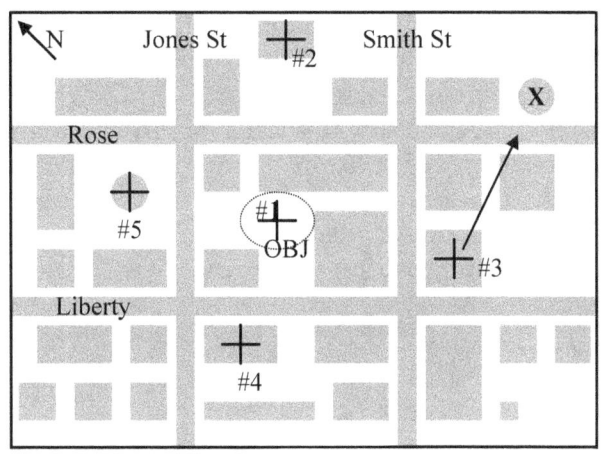

Figure IV-4. Target Reference Points

"TRP #3, 087 degrees magnetic, 325 meters, the water tower."

5. Target Marking and Friendly Positions

The close proximity of friendly forces to targets makes positively locating and marking of both friendly units and targets critical. Procedures must be clearly understood and all participants must be issued the appropriate devices. All fire support assets should be familiar with the friendly marking system. The methods to do this are limited only by the creativity of the ground forces and aircrews. Commanders should use this section as a reference and not limit themselves to only these methods. Aircrews require positive location of the target and friendly positions before expending ordnance. Methods employed must be adapted to the existing conditions. Positive air to ground communications are essential to coordinate and authenticate markings. Table IV-1 lists some common marking methods and describes their merits and shortcomings. All personnel must understand both the strengths and weaknesses of available methods and equipment and how they pertain to urban conditions. They need to choose the appropriate method, equipment or equipment combination for the conditions at hand. The following sections address several factors to consider when using target marking methods and equipment.

a. Aircrews and terminal controllers must become familiar with the roof characteristics of buildings before a mission since this often will be the first characteristic used for identification by aircrew. Flat roofs, pitched roofs, domed roofs, roofs with towers or air conditioning units on top will aid in visual and thermal acquisition. Additional structural features revealed in imagery will aid in confirmation. This method of terrain association will prove invaluable for visual engagement or reconnaissance since structures are often too close for relying on mere grid coordinates.

b. The visual signaling or marking of positions allows more ease in determining the location of friendly forces. During building clearing operations, the progress of friendly units (both horizontally and vertically) may be marked with spray paint or bed sheets hung out of windows. Often, the simplest methods are the best. Traditional signaling devices, such as flares, strobes, and signaling mirrors may be effective as well. Target marking or an orientation on enemy positions may also be accomplished using signaling procedures. Common techniques include the use of smoke, laser pointer devices, or tracers (Table IV-1). Devices are available which aid in the recognition of friendly forces under difficult battlefield conditions. Fluid tactical situations, intermingling of forces, and urban terrain all contribute to difficulty in identifying friendly troops and equipment. The use of GLINT tape, combat ID panels, and IR beacons assist in the ID of friendly ground forces on urban terrain. Standardized usage of ground lighting, thermal contrast, and interposition of structures influence the effectiveness of these devices.

Table IV-1. Target and Friendly Marking Methods

METHOD	DAY/ NIGHT	ASSETS	FRIENDLY MARKS	TARGET MARKS	REMARKS
SMOKE	D/N	ALL	GOOD	GOOD	Easily identifiable, may compromise friendly position, obscure target, or warn of fire support employment. Placement may be difficult due to structures.
SMOKE (IR)	D/N	ALL NVD AT NIGHT	GOOD	GOOD	Easily identifiable, may compromise friendly position, obscure target, or warn of fire support employment. Placement may be difficult due to structures. Night marking is greatly enhanced by the use of IR reflective smoke
ILLUM, GROUND BURST	D/N	ALL	N/A	GOOD	Easily identified, may wash out NVD's.
SIGNAL MIRROR	D	ALL	GOOD	N/A	Avoids compromise of friendly location. Dependent on weather and available light and may be lost in reflections from other reflective surfaces (windshields, windows, water, etc.)
SPOT LIGHT	N	ALL	GOOD	MARGINAL	Highly visible to all. Compromises friendly position and warns of fire support employment. Effectiveness is dependent upon degree of urban lighting.
IR SPOT LIGHT	N	ALL NVD	GOOD	MARGINAL	Visible to all with NVG's. Less likely to compromise than overt light. Effectiveness dependent upon degree of urban lighting.
IR LASER POINTER (below .4 watts)	N	ALL NVD	GOOD	MARGINAL	Effectiveness dependent upon degree of urban lighting.
IR LASER POINTER (above .4 watts)	N	ALL NVD	GOOD	GOOD	Less affected by ambient light and weather conditions. Highly effective under all but the most highly lit or worst weather conditions. IZLID-2 is the current example.
VISUAL LASER	N	ALL	GOOD	MARGINAL	Highly visible to all. Risk of compromise is high. Effectiveness dependant upon degree of urban lighting.
LASER DESIGNATOR	D/N	PGM OR LST EQUIPED	N/A	GOOD	Highly effective with PGM. Very restrictive laser acquisition cone and requires line of sight to target. May require pre-coordination of laser codes
TRACER	D/N	ALL	N/A	MARGINAL	May compromise position. May be difficult to distinguish mark from other gunfire. During daytime use, may be more effective to kick up dust surrounding target.
ELECTRONIC BEACON	D/N	SEE REMARKS	EXCELLENT	GOOD	Ideal friendly marking device for AC-130 and some USAF fixed wing (not compatible with Navy or Marine aircraft). Least impeded by urban terrain. Can be used as a TRP for target identification. Coordination with aircrews essential to ensure equipment and training compatibility.
STROBE (OVERT)	N	ALL	MARGINAL	N/A	Visible by all. Effectiveness dependent upon degree of urban lighting.
STROBE (IR)	N	ALL NVD	GOOD	N/A	Visible to all NVDs. Effectiveness dependent upon degree of urban lighting. Coded strobes aid in acquisition
FLARE (OVERT)	D/N	ALL	GOOD	N/A	Visible by all. Easily identified by aircrew.
FLARE (IR)	N	ALL NVD	GOOD	N/A	Visible to all NVDs. Easily identified by aircrew.
GLINT/IR PANEL	N	ALL NVD	GOOD	N/A	Not readily detectable by enemy. Very effective except in highly lit areas.
COMBAT IDENTIFICATION PANEL	D/N	ALL FLIR	GOOD	N/A	Provides temperature contrast on vehicles or building. May be obscured by urban terrain.
VS-17 PANEL	D	ALL	MARGINAL	N/A	Only visible during daylight. Easily obscured by structures.
CHEMICAL HEAT SOURCES	D/N	ALL FLIR	POOR	N/A	Easily masked by urban structures and lost in thermal clutter. Difficult to acquire, can be effective when used to contrast cold background or when a/c knows general location.
SPINNING CHEM LIGHT (OVERT)	N	ALL	MARGINAL	N/A	Provides unique signature. May be obscured by structures. Provides a distinct signature easily recognized. Effectiveness dependent upon degree of urban lighting.
SPINNING CHEM LIGHT (IR)	N	ALL NVD	MARGINAL	N/A	Provides unique signature. May be obscured by structures. Effectiveness dependent upon degree of urban lighting.

c. During both high and low ambient light conditions, expect to see significant urban shadowing from buildings when cultural lights are present. Shadows will hide personnel and/or vehicular targets from both the terminal guidance controller and the aircrew like the shadows that hide small hills against the background of larger mountains. Shadows will hide non-thermally significant targets, but thermal targets still can be seen. When a combination of sensors has to be used to acquire and identify the target, a sensor hand-off plan must be briefed thoroughly. The use of aircraft with integrated GPS will reduce the amount of time spent finding the target area. Time permitting, inputting a target grid into the GPS or inertial navigation system (INS) will provide fire control cues (range, heading, time) to the target that will aid in quicker target acquisition and help distinguish friendly forces from enemy forces. Because CAS missions may involve short firing ranges, expect a minimum tracking time, and thus, minimum time to optimize the sensor.

6. Television/Electro-optical (TV/EO)

TV/EO sensors are subject to many of the same limitations as the naked eye, particularly TV with no low light capability. Aircrews will encounter difficulties in acquiring a target and achieving lock-on if smoke, buildings, or other urban factors repeatedly interrupt LOS. Low light or all light TV/EO sensors may require frequent gain and filter changes to accommodate varying light levels in urban areas. Normal means of target and friendly ID are likely to prove ineffective. IR strobes, overt strobes, and laser pointers normally visible to TV/EO sensors can be lost in the light clutter. Typical TV/EO resolution is not sufficient at medium and extended ranges to discriminate between a friendly position or a target and its surrounding urban features. Ground personnel need to utilize more aggressive and overt means of identifying their position and that of the target if TV/EO sensors are to be used to identify, track and engage targets on urban terrain.

7. Electronic Beacons

Electronic beacons can be an effective tool for friendly ID in an urban environment, especially when friendly troops are on the move. However, a significant drawback to beacons is that only a few aircraft can track them. When other means of ID prove time consuming, a beacon may help locate a friendly position quickly. When a friendly ground team is on the move, no matter whether on foot or in a vehicle, a beacon offers a good way to track the movement. When LOS is repeatedly interrupted, a beacon tracking radar can temporarily break lock from the friendly position. However, when LOS is reestablished, the beacon tracking radar can reacquire the friendly troops. Further, when urban terrain prevents visual contact with a friendly position, target location can be passed via reference to a beacon. If necessary, an aircraft can attack a target with nothing more than an offset from the beacon. This method should only be employed as a last resort since it will not provide the precision normally desired in an urban environment.

8. Laser Designation

a. Background. One of the greatest challenges for an aircraft in urban terrain is achieving and maintaining LOS with a target or friendly position. Laser designation requires uninterrupted LOS to identify and engage a target. Rotary-wing aircraft may use their hover capabilities, but only in the most permissive environments. This may mean a rotary-wing lasing platform has to be very near the target to keep the spot on the target until ordnance impact. Smoke from burning buildings or other fires can drift across the laser to target line causing beam attenuation. While this is also true on an open battlefield, urban areas typically contain more potential smoke sources than found in natural terrain.

b. Lasers. Most laser designating platforms cannot actually see their laser spot on a target. Lasers are often boresighted to other supporting sensors like FLIR/IDS or TV/EO. If the supporting sensor cannot see a target, then the laser cannot effectively mark the target. Furthermore, although a FLIR/IDS can "see" a target, the laser may not be capable of guiding ordnance against it since smoke, invisible to the FLIR/IDS, can effectively attenuate the laser energy. The most important factor affecting FLIR performance is water vapor concentration, which is indicated by high relative humidity, and expressed by absolute humidity. The impact of high water vapor concentration (indicated by high humidity) is greater on FLIR/IDS performance than its impact on laser performance. In other words, if the target can be detected with a FLIR in clear air, then the laser should provide sufficient energy for seeker acquisition. As a rule of thumb, if a target can be detected with a supporting sensor and consistently ranged to with a laser, it is likely that the laser will designate satisfactorily for a laser-guided weapon. As an additional consideration, many targets are relatively small and can only be acquired at relatively short range. For low and medium threats, where a great amount of time is available to use the FLIR/IDS to point the laser, target acquisition methods are simple. As the threat escalates and the time available for target acquisition shrinks, targeting with the FLIR/IDS becomes more difficult.

9. Clearance to Drop/Fire for CAS Missions

a. Background. The responsibility for ordnance delivery rests with the maneuver force commander. The terminal controller has the authority to clear aircraft to release weapons after specific or general release approval from the maneuver force commander. For specific guidance see Joint Publication (JP) 3-09.3, JTTP for Close Air Support, Chapter 5. Additional references are the MTTP found in FM 90-20, MCRP 3-16.8B, NWP 3-09.2, and AFTTP(I) 3-2.6, J-Fire, Multiservice Procedures for the Joint Application of Firepower.

b. Positive control. Positive control will be used to the maximum extent possible. For specific guidance, refer to JP 3-09.3, Chapter 5. Additional references are the MTTP found in FM 90-20, MCRP 3-16.8B, NWP 3-09.2, and AFTTP(I) 3-2.6, J-Fire, Multiservice Procedures for the Joint Application of Firepower.

c. Reasonable Assurance. Aircrews normally operate under positive control and receive a "cleared hot" before releasing ordnance in a CAS environment. During combat operations, low altitude flight, and deteriorating battlefield conditions, such as communications jamming, can prevent the receipt of positive clearance. JP 3-09.3 recommends that a joint force commander (JFC) establish guidelines that allow CAS missions to be conducted utilizing reasonable assurance. Reasonable assurance is not a routine procedure but a set of specific guidelines. It is not a "comm out" method of attack. The JFC establishes the conditions for reasonable assurance and when they will be in effect.

d. Risk-Estimate Distances. Risk-estimate distances are based on fragmentation patterns and allow the ground forces commander or combat air commander to estimate the risk in terms of the percent of friendly casualties that may result from an air strike against an enemy threat along the forward line of own troops. First and foremost, all aircrews must understand their aircraft weapons' capabilities and limitations. Secondly, the ground commander must have a clearly defined intent and ROE that is understood by all aircrews to ensure the proper matching of weapons to targets.

NOTE: The recommended probability of incapacitation (Pi) distances from friendly troops assumes flat open terrain, not urban terrain with buildings for cover and vertical structures that may mask the effects of ordnance fragment patterns. In some cases, closer delivery can be made if terrain (friendly cover) permits or if the tactical situation is urgent. The forward air controller (FAC) shall inform the ground unit commander of the risks involved before commencing such a strike.

---

10. Fixed-wing Targeting and Engagements (AV-8B, A-10, O/A-10, F-14, F-15E, F-16, F/A-18, and F-117)

a. Targeting and engagements. The standard 9 line, CAS control brief will be the preferred method of controlling fixed-wing aircraft when conducting CAS. The available weapons suites for selected fixed-wing aircraft are shown in Table IV-2.

Table IV-2. Fixed-wing Weapons Suites

Aircraft M/D/S	Using Service	Ordnance	Laser Capability LST	Laser Capability LTD	Marking Capability	Beacon Capability	Other Systems
AV-8B	USMC	LGBs Maverick GP Bombs CBUs 2.75" Rockets 5.00" Rockets Napalm 25mm cannon AGM-122 Sidearm	YES	NO	Rockets 25mm HEI rounds LUU-2 Flares	None	TV GPS NVG
AV-8B "Plus"	USMC	As Above	YES	NO	Rockets	None	NVG FLIR Radar
A/OA-10A	USAF	Maverick GP Bombs CBUs HE rockets 30mm cannon	YES	NO	WP Rockets 30mm HEI IR pointer LUU-1/2 LUU-5/6 LUU-19 M257 IR Rockets M278 Covert Rockets	None	NVG
F-14	USN	LGBs GP Bombs CBUs 20mm cannon Aerial mines	NO	YES	Laser WP LUU-2 Flares	None	NVG Radar TGP LLTV
F-15E	USAF	LGBs AGM-130 GBU-15 Maverick GP Bombs CBUs 20mm cannon	NO	YES	Laser 20mm HEI rounds	PPN-19 PPN-20 UPN-25/34 TPN-23/26 SST-181 X/XE PRD-78/80 SMP-1000	NVG FLIR TGP Radar
F-16 C (less LANTIRN)	USAF	LGBs Maverick GP Bombs CBUs 20mm cannon	YES (Some)	NO	Laser (some) WP rockets 20mm HEI rounds	PPN-19 PPN-20 UPN-25/34 TPN-23/26 SST-181 X/XE PRD-78/80 SMP-1000	Radar NVG TGP (some) SADL (some)
F-16CG (with LANTIRN)	USAF	LGBs Maverick GP Bombs CBUs 20mm cannon	NO	YES	Laser WP Rockets 20mm HEI rounds	PPN-19 PPN-20 UPN-25/34 TPN-23/26 SST-181 X/XE PRD-78/80 SMP-1000	NVG FLIR TGP Radar GPS IDM
F-16CJ	USAF	HARM JDAM Maverick GP Bombs CBUs 20mm cannon JSOW	NO	NO	20mm HEI	PPN-19 PPN-20 UPN-25/34 TPN-23/26 SST-181 X/XE PRD-78/80 SMP-1000	NVG Radar GPS IDM HTS
F/A-18	USN (A/C) USMC (A/C/D)	LGBs Maverick SLAM HARM GP Bombs CBUs 2.75" Rockets 5.00" Rockets Napalm/FAE 20mm cannon Laser Maverick JSOW JDAM	YES	YES	Laser WP Rockets HE Rockets LUU-2 Flares 20mm HEI rounds IR Pointer (F/A-18D only)	None	FLIR GPS NVG Radar

Notes:
1. All fixed-wing aircraft shown also have aerial missiles
2. All aircraft that drop CBUs can also drop aerial mines

b. Roles. Fixed-wing aircraft can be employed in the following roles:

(1) Offensive Counter Air (OCA),

(2) Defensive Counter Air (DCA),

(3) Strategic Attack,

(4) CAS,

(5) Interdiction,

(6) Armed Reconnaissance,

(7) Escort,

(8) Airborne FAC [FAC(A)],

(9) SEAD,

(10) Supporting Arms Coordinator, Airborne [SAC(A)].

c. Employment. Not all of the previously mentioned fixed-wing employment missions will be used in all urban operations. More information on OCA and DCA missions can be found in JP 3-01, Joint Doctrine for Countering Air and Missile Threats; furthermore, strategic attack, interdiction, and escort may be found in JP 3-03, Doctrine for Joint Interdiction Operations. Lastly SEAD missions are discussed in JP 3-01.4, Joint Suppression of Enemy Air Defenses. The fixed-wing missions addressed in this section are armed reconnaissance, FAC(A), and CAS.

(1) Armed Reconnaissance. In the armed reconnaissance mission, the tasked aircraft take off with no assigned target to attack. Instead, they are given a designated sector. They conduct the reconnaissance in advance of ground forces. Potential targets might include reserves, logistic centers, C2 facilities, bridges, and railroads.

(2) FAC(A). The FAC(A) mission has advantages because of the potentially restricted LOS that a ground FAC encounters. The FAC(A) may be able to better position himself to mark a target for attacking aircraft. The FAC(A) also has the same vantage point of the target area as the attacking aircraft.

(3) CAS. Fixed-wing aircraft tasked with CAS provide timely, precision-delivered ordnance that can mean the difference between victory and defeat. CAS has a devastating effect upon the enemy. Both his morale and will to fight are affected. Target acquisition and location will be the most difficult aspects of urban fixed-wing CAS.

11. Fixed-wing Targeting and Engagements (AC-130)

a. Background. In a typical AC-130 CAS mission, the aircraft places fire against targets in close proximity to friendly forces. CAS engagement distances may be reduced to "danger close," which is that distance producing a 0.1 percent Pi based on USAF 61A1-3-4, JMEM data. For the AC-130's weapons, danger close is 200 meters (m) for the 105 millimeter (mm) and 125 m for the 40mm and 25mm. For engagements inside danger close, the ground commander must accept responsibility for the increased potential for injury to his troops. Engagements on urban terrain may be well inside danger close distances. In fact, many may be at less than 50 m.

b. Marking Friendly Forces. The most important step in any CAS engagement is to locate the friendly forces. This is doctrinally accomplished with some type of marking that can be seen visually from the aircraft or observed using the aircraft sensors. In an urban environment, the ambient lighting may obscure the marking. This makes some other form of marking necessary, such as IR sensors or electronic beacons.

(1) IR Sensors. IR chemlights, MRE heaters, space blankets, and temperature absorbing panels provide markings significant to IDS or low light level TV systems.

(2) Electronic Beacons. The currently fielded PPN-19 radar beacon is large and heavy, making it burdensome for lightly equipped, fast moving troops. However, a new micro-transponder, the smaller selectable strike (SST)-201, is being fielded to provide a usable radar beacon that is lightweight and easily employed. This capability can be used to locate the friendly forces and orient the sensors to the target for a direct engagement. It can also be used as a fire control offset to engage the target.

c. Locating the Target. Locating the target usually is accomplished by locating the friendly forces first. From the friendly location, a bearing and range offset is often used to orient the AC-130 to the target area. From the target description, the gunship attempts to positively identify the target. In urban terrain, a detailed talk-on with reference points expedites target acquisition. Another very effective technique is for the friendly team to designate the target with an IR target designator, like the laser pointer long range (LPL)-30. This is the most expeditious and accurate method of target confirmation. Again, ambient lights in the urban environment may obscure the marker. The HC-130H gunship is equipped with an infrared zoom laser illuminator designator (IZLID) to aid in target confirmation. The gated laser illuminator casts a very large and diffused IR spot on the target area. Whatever the method, target confirmation is crucial to eliminate fratricide and collateral damage.

d. Roles. The AC-130H/U is ideally suited for fire support in low threat urban environments. Within permissive environments, the AC-130H/U is effective in the following roles:

(1) CAS-primary mission,

(2) Interdiction,

(3) Armed reconnaissance,

(4) Point defense,

(5) Escort,

(6) Surveillance,

(7) LZ/PZ/DZ security support,

(8) Airborne C2 (limited),

(9) Search and rescue (SAR) support.

e. Aircraft Systems. A full array of imaging and target designation systems, precision navigation and secure communications equipment, and a defensive avionics suite is standard. Additionally, the APQ-180 navigation/fire control radar (AC-130U) offers adverse weather delivery capability. The weapons suite aboard the AC-130H/U includes items in the Table IV-3.

Table IV-3. AC-130H/U Weapons Suite

Aircraft M/D/S	Using Service	Ordnance	Laser Capability LST	Laser Capability LTD	Marking Capability	Beacon Capability	Other Systems
AC-130H	USAF	M2A1 Modified 40mm M-102 105mm	NO	YES 1688 ONLY	LTD/R GLINT IZLID-2 40mm 105mm	PPN-19 UPN-25 SST-181 SST-201	NVG FLIR LLLTV GPS INS APQ-150
AC-130U	USAF	GAU-12U 25mm M2A1 Modified 40mm M-102 105mm	NO	YES	LTD/R GLINT 40mm 105mm	PPN-19 UPN-25 SST-181 SST-201	NVG FLIR ALLTV GPS INS APQ-180

f. Weapons Data. Weapons applicability, delivery altitude, munitions data are included in Table IV-4.

Table IV-4. AC-130H/U Weapons Applicability

Weapon	Target Types	Min/Max Alt (AGL)	Rds/Min	Combat Load	Remarks
25mm	Pers under light cover & light vehicles	3000/15000'	1800	3000	HEI
40mm	Pers under medium cover & all light vehicles	4500/18000'	100	256/500*	HEI API HEI-P
105mm	Pers, light vehicles, & buildings	4500/20000'	10-Jun	100/174*	HE (point detonate or delay) HEHF
* If equipped with additional ammunition rack. (AC-130H)					

g. Call For Fire. The call for fire method for AC-130s differs from the standard CAS "nine-line". Five lines of data are passed, as follows:

(1) Observer/warning order,

(2) Friendly location/mark,

(3) Target location,

(4) Target description/mark,

(5) Remarks (Include threats to gunship).

12. Rotary-wing Targeting and Engagements (AH-1, AH-1W, AH-6, AH-64, MH-60, OH-58D, UH-1N)

a. Targeting and engagements. The standard 9 line, CAS control brief will be the preferred method of controlling rotary-wing aircraft when conducting CAS engagements. The available weapons suites for selected rotary-wing aircraft are shown in Table IV-5.

Table IV-5. Rotary-wing Weapons Suites

Aircraft M/D/S	Using Service	Ordnance	Laser Capability LST	Laser Capability LTD	Marking Capability	Beacon Capability	Other Systems
AH-1	USA	TOW 2.75" Rockets 20mm	YES	NO	WP Rockets	None	NVG
AH-1W	USMC	Hellfire TOW Sidewinder Sidearm 5" Rockets 2.75" Rockets 20mm	NO	YES	Rockets WP LASER	None	NVG CCDTV FLIR (with organic CCDTV system) GPS DVO
AH-6	USA (SOF)	Hellfire 2.75" Rockets .50 Caliber 7.62mm Minigun	NO	YES	WP Smoke LASER	None	NVG FLIR GPS
AH-64	USA	Hellfire 2.75" Rockets 30mm HEDP Stinger	YES	YES	WP Smoke LASER	None	NVG FLIR GPS DTV
MH-60	USA (SOF)	Hellfire 30mm HEDP 2.75" Rockets .50 Caliber 7.62mm Minigun	NO	YES	None Smoke LASER	None	NVG FLIR GPS
OH-58D	USA	Hellfire 2.75" Rockets .50 Caliber Stinger	NO	YES	WP Smoke LASER	None	NVG FLIR GPS DTV
UH-1N	USMC	2.75" Rockets .50 Caliber 7.62mm minigun	NO	NO	WP	None	NVG FLIR GPS
MH-53	USAF (SOF)	.50 Caliber 7.62 Minigun	NO	NO	None	None	NVG FLIR GPS TFTA
HH-60	USAF	7.62mm Minigun	NO	NO	None	None	NVG FLIR GPS

b. Roles. Rotary-wing aircraft can be employed in the following roles:

(1) CAS,

(2) Interdiction,

(3) Armed reconnaissance,

(4) Escort,

(5) FAC(A),

(6) SEAD,

(7) Assault support,

(8) Logistic support,

(9) C2,

(10) Combat SAR (CSAR),

(11) Airmobile assault,

(12) Medical evacuation (MEDEVAC).

c. Running/diving fire. Rotary-wing aircraft should make running and diving fire engagements along corridors of visibility. These engagements require continuous movement to minimize exposure time. Before unmasking, all weapons should be configured and armed. In situations where only one aircraft at a time is in a position to engage, the lead aircraft fires as soon as possible after achieving a firing solution, then a break turn is made toward masking terrain immediately after firing. The wingman provides suppression when lead makes the break. Avoid flight into other target visibility corridors during the egress. Re-attacks should be from alternate directions to avoid predictability. (Figure IV-5)

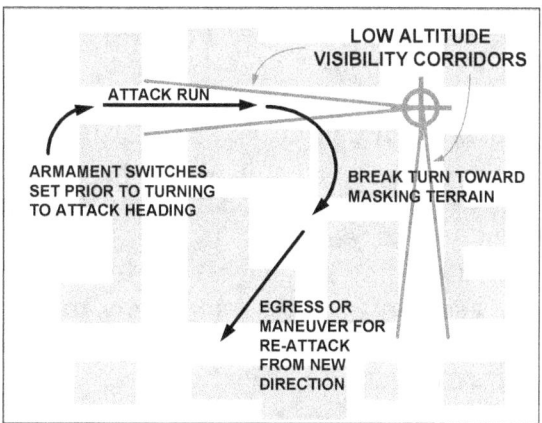

Figure IV-5. Running/Diving Fire Engagement

d. Hover Fire. Hovering fire engagements are not recommended, but may be made. The normal considerations apply for the selection of firing positions. Buildings and structures, which offer cover and concealment from the target area, are treated like natural terrain. It must again be emphasized, however, that all urban features are potential enemy positions. Features selected for vertical unmasking should not be significantly taller than surrounding structures. They should be selected to provide target visibility at the lowest possible altitude. Many rotary-wing engagements will be conducted at very close ranges (<500m), often inside the minimum range for the Hellfire missile. At such close ranges, use of the cannon is highly recommended. Minimize the time spent stationary in the position. Plan multiple firing points and egress routes providing maximum cover and concealment. (Figure IV-6) Second to enemy fire, wire and tower obstacles will present the biggest hazard to flight when pulling off a target run in the urban environment.

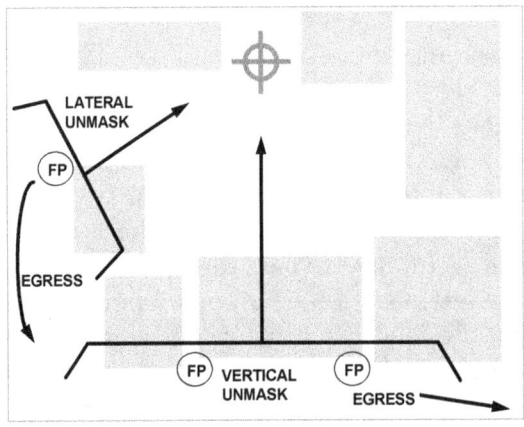

Figure IV-6. Hover Fire Engagement

13. Artillery, Mortars, and Naval Surface Fire Support (NSFS)

a. Background. Artillery, mortars, and NSFS are used in aviation urban operations for target marking, illumination, and SEAD. Marking smoke may be white phosphorus (WP), red phosphorus, or illumination rounds set for ground burst. Illumination rounds provide additional light to aid in night operations. They are used to illuminate areas of suspected enemy activity, provide direction, mark targets, or "wash out" enemy passive NVD when used at ground level. IR illumination rounds are especially effective in urban areas devoid of artificial light sources. Planning must ensure that aircrews will be flying with NVG. However, balance using illumination rounds for target marking with the high potential for creating unwanted smoke and fires. Mortars are ideally suited for SEAD because of their high angle fire. This is especially true against highly mobile MANPADS that are often employed from rooftops.

(1) Artillery. Artillery can be effective in an urban environment because of the capability for high trajectory firing. High-angle fire is required when firing from or within built-up areas, or over high terrain features. However, positioning artillery units in the urban environment creates additional airspace deconfliction concerns due to the high-angle firing requirement. The observer must also realize that there is increased dispersion during high-angle fire. Some of the most effective types of projectiles and fuzes are as follows:

(a) Copperhead. Copperhead is a 155-mm cannon-launched guided projectile with a shaped charge warhead and a laser seeker. Copperhead homes in on laser energy reflected from the target during the final portion of its trajectory. Copperhead should be used only when direct fire systems are unable to engage. Fire planning for Copperhead should consider the engagement ranges of the laser designator. Moving targets can normally be engaged out to approximately 3 kilometers (km), while stationary targets can be engaged out to 5 km. Laser designation requires an uninterrupted line of sight between the designator and the target. Any obstructions weaken the laser signal causing a decrease in the performance of the Copperhead round. Copperhead engagements must be carefully analyzed for effects of the gun-target line, observer-target line, and masking effects of surrounding structures during the terminal guidance phase of trajectory.

(b) Delay fuzing. Required for penetration of reinforced or hardened rooftops.

(c) Variable time (VT) fusing. Required for an airburst. Effective in clearing rooftops, but has greater potential for collateral damage.

(2) Mortars. Mortars are generally very effective in urban terrain due to their high angle trajectories. Several systems are available depending on the ground units involved in the operation. These systems include:

(a) 60-mm Mortar. The (M224) 60-mm mortar is in Army airborne, air assault, light infantry, and ranger companies and all Marine rifle companies. The current family of ammunition consists of high explosive (HE), smoke, illumination, and IR illumination.

(b) 81-mm Mortar. The (M252) 81-mm mortar is in all Marine infantry, and Army light battalions. The current family of ammunition consists of HE, smoke (Red phosphorus), illumination, and IR illumination.

(c) 120-mm Mortar. The 120-mm mortar is fielded in a heavy Army battalion. The current family of ammunition consists of HE, smoke, and illumination, and IR Illumination.

(3) NSFS. When available, NSFS provides effective fire support to forces operating near coastal waters. However, equipment limitations, enemy electronic warfare, and unfavorable atmospheric conditions can interrupt radio communications to control NSFS. Naval guns are not normally suitable for high-angle fire because of their high muzzle velocity.

(a) NSFS ships normally remain under control of the Commander, Amphibious Task Force (CATF). Ship positioning and method of delivery remain with the ship captain. When the ships are threatened, the target-attack priorities of the ship may cause it to hold or cancel land force fire missions until the threat is removed.

(b) NSFS ships are normally assigned one of two missions: direct support or general support. A ship in direct support delivers both planned and on-call fires. General support missions are assigned to ships supporting forces of brigade size and larger. The supported force selects the targets, the timing of fires, and the method of adjustment of fires.

(c) NSFS has a variety of weapons ranging from conventional armament to missiles. NSFS ships also have a large variety of ammunition and high rates of fire, allowing them to attack a variety of targets. The ships are mobile, allowing positioning to take advantage of their limited deflection pattern.

(d) Close supporting fire is most effective when the gun-target line is parallel to friendly front lines. The relatively flat trajectory of naval gunfire results in a large range probable error. Hydrographic conditions may cause the ship to take up firing positions that cause the gun-target line to be perpendicular to friendly front lines. When this change in the gun-target line happens, it makes naval gunfire less suitable to engage targets close to friendly troops.

14. Close Air Support

CAS requests consist of two types: preplanned and immediate. Preplanned CAS requests are further divided into scheduled and on-call, which are processed in ample time to provide the munitions required. On the other hand, immediate requests provide the munitions available, which may not be the most suitable. Immediate CAS performed under the control of a non-qualified controller is called Emergency CAS. Careful consideration and SOPs on how to conduct emergency CAS are necessary. Decentralized execution is critical; however, personnel at all levels need to be ready to assist and clarify whenever possible. Ideally, match the simplest means available to control the aircraft with the controllers' requirements. Aircrews and other supporting personnel may need to pull information from the controller. Taking the extra time to build a clear picture of the situation increases the odds of mission success. For additional guidance, refer to JP 3-09.3. Additional references are the MTTP found in FM 90-20, MCRP 3-16.8B, NWP 3-09.2, and AFTTP(I) 3-2.6, J-Fire, Multiservice Procedures for the Joint Application of Firepower.

15. Munitions Effectiveness

a. Background. Analyzing the effects that munitions will have on buildings is an important consideration in urban operations. Modern construction and design improvements provide many buildings with resiliency to the blast effects of bomb and artillery attack. Although modern buildings may burn easily, they often retain their structural integrity and remain standing. A large, modern structure can take between 24 to 48 hours to burn out. Once buildings become skeletal, they are still useful to the military. Table IV-6 summarizes the general characteristics of building materials worldwide and can be useful when determining the proper munitions to employ.

Table IV-6. Wall Thickness and Incidence of Occurrence of Building Types

Building Type	Wall Thickness Centimeter (cm)	Occurrence All Building Types (%)
Mass Construction (Load Bearing Outer Walls) Stone	75	0.6
Brick	34-65	62.9
Reinforced concrete (Poured-in-Place Tilt-Up Combination)	15-25	6.1
Bow-Wall Principle	15-25	0.8
Framed(Nonload-Bearing Walls) Wood	15	15.8
Steel/Concrete Heavy/Cladding	36	1.8
Steel/Concrete Light/Cladding	17	12.0

b. Weaponeering. The JMEM defines specific weaponeering procedures to accomplish this analysis. The weaponeering process can be quite involved and requires training. Expedient models can be developed based on preliminary analysis of generic targets. Mission planners should be most concerned with the factors of blast effects, fragmentation, and circular error probable (CEP). CEP is an indicator of the delivery accuracy of a weapon system and is used as a factor in determining the probable damage to a target. Information specific to all these planning factors is found in the JMEM. Specifics of weapon penetration, accuracy and performance can be calculated quickly and easily. In addition, rough estimates of possible collateral damage can be determined using the target offset portion of the JMEM algorithms. The JMEM does not produce collateral weapons effects on friendly personnel in close proximity and shielded by some form of structure. The Joint Warfare Assessment Center (JWAC) located at Dahlgren, Virginia, performs classified computer simulations for these situations. Although primarily tasked by the theater commander for deliberate targeting, they can provide to any user the weapons effect characteristics in an urban area for general-purpose bombs, laser-guided bombs, Maverick missiles, and high-speed anti-radiation missile (HARM). Send a request for information via Joint Deployable Intelligence Support System (JDISS) (www@jwac.ic.gov) or by telephone, Defense Switched Network (DSN): 249-1992/4587. They require at a minimum: scene composition, aimpoints, attack direction, weapon/fuze combination, and time over target. Additionally, using the collateral damage estimate tool (CDET), JWAC can provide glass breakage plots, eardrum rupture plots (friendly, enemy, and non-combatant concerns), and panel damage versus distance from impact point.

16. Munitions Delivery

a. Background. Urban terrain introduces a unique challenge to aircrews and ground personnel alike with the notion of the urban canyon. Simply stated, an urban canyon exists when a target or target set is shielded by vertical structures. Unlike most natural terrain, the vertical characteristics of urban terrain can greatly affect delivery options.

b. LOS. Urban terrain typically creates corridors of visibility running between structures. Street level targets are only visible along the street axis or from high angles. The interposition of structures around a target interrupts LOS from many directions. Rooftop targets may be approachable from a wider range of azimuths. Targeting a specific face and story of a building can limit engagement heading. The presence of buildings and other structures in urban terrain creates corridors of visibility along streets, rivers, and railways. Achieving LOS with an objective at street level is much easier along the axis of the roadway as opposed to perpendicular. Large cities in particular create a canyon effect in terms of visibility. Look down is required into areas surrounded by tall structures if roadways do not create an adequate avenue of observation. (Figure IV-7)

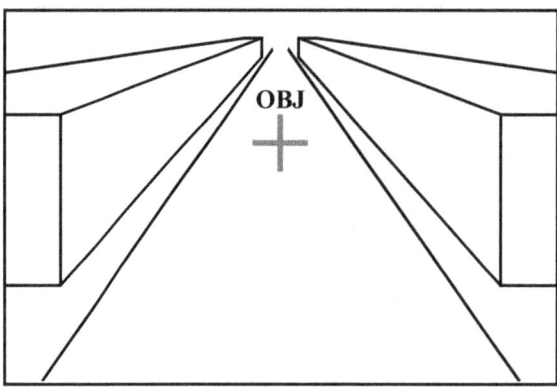

Figure IV-7. View Along Street (Low angle possible)

c. Employment Range. The employment range for ordnance from both fixed-, and rotary-wing aircraft is significantly reduced in urban areas. Delivery of direct fire weapons is typically at medium to close range, due to masking effects of city structures. The amount of sensor depression required to achieve LOS with an objective is called look-down. The look-down angle required to achieve LOS with an area is determined based on the lateral distance to masking structures and the height of those structures. There may be an increase in minimum engagement ranges because of high look down angles, thus making many close engagements possible. The higher the aircraft above the intended target the more stand off is needed. Fields of fire tend to be very narrow for the same reason. Often only one aircraft at a time can be in a position suitable for engagement of the target. Higher angle deliveries may provide better look angles and visibility into a target area as well as a better ballistic trajectory when delivering ordnance near tall structures. See Figures IV-8 and IV-9.

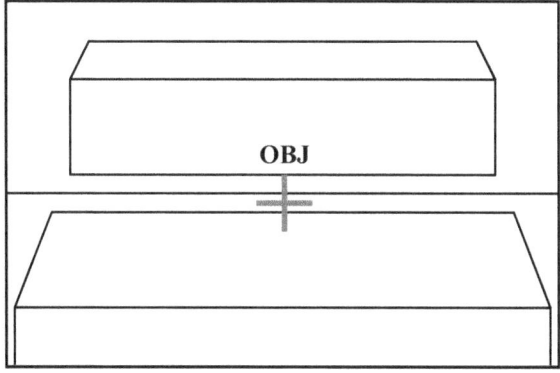

Figure IV-8. Look-Down View (Greater angle required)

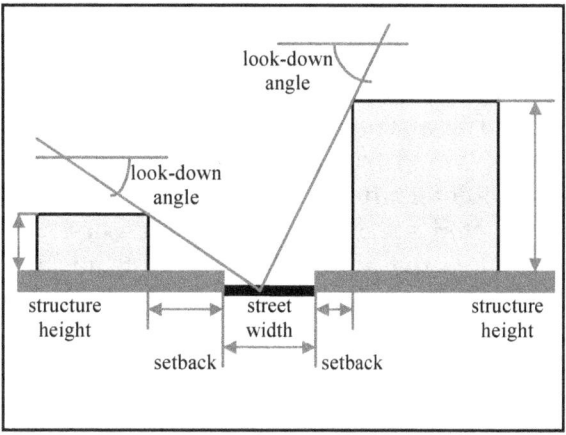

Figure IV-9. Look-Down Angle

The central problem lies in maintaining LOS to the intended target with enough time to acquire the target, achieve a weapons delivery solution, and fly to those parameters. Visibility limitations on marking devices in the urban environment are geometric in nature. The use of any pointer or laser requires LOS. In addition, the aircraft must have LOS with the target to see the mark. Urban terrain severely limits LOS opportunities. Due to the close proximity of structures to one another, there may be very narrow fields of view and limited axes of approach. The high number of reflective surfaces in an urban setting presents an additional challenge. Laser energy can be reflected and present multiple false returns. For these reasons, urban fire support can be expected to be more time consuming and be much more dependent on good communications. Combinations of marking devices and clear talk-on procedures will be essential to safe and effective fire support.

    d. Lasing Techniques. Aircrews should consider using buddy lasing or remote lasing tactics for laser-guided munitions when urban effects preclude the attacking aircraft from maintaining LOS with the target until ordnance impact.

However, if designating with a ground based laser along a narrow street bounded by tall buildings, LOS geometry may allow the weapon to receive reflected laser energy only within the 20 degree safety zone; the area from which a weapon should not be released normally. As in any delivery, aircrews must consider the target, the threat, the weapon, and the weather. Aircrews must also consider the potential miss distances for "precision" munitions when their guidance source is interrupted or removed.

e. Delivery Parameters. Several factors will drive the aircrew's selection of delivery parameters for a given weapon in urban terrain. Many deliveries tend to limit avenues of approach due to LOS requirements between the aircraft and target. The presence of buildings and other structures in urban terrain creates corridors of visibility along streets, rivers, and railways. Achieving LOS with an objective at lower altitudes is much easier along the axis of the roadway rather than perpendicular to it. Large cities, in particular, create a canyon effect in terms of visibility. Areas surrounded by tall structures must be looked down into if roadways do not create an adequate avenue of observation.

f. Run-in. When working with a FAC or tactical air control party/post (TACP), suggested run-in headings should be given that allow the maximum probability of target ID. The aircrew should build a mental image of the target before ingress so that target and friendly location is facilitated. If possible, a dry pass may be warranted to determine if proper LOS requirements can be met for employment with the selected set of delivery parameters. Other factors such as threats or weather may force the aircraft to deliver from low altitude. This increases the importance of attacking from a sufficient avenue of approach to allow target ID and weapons employment given the inherent LOS limitations.

g. Proximity of Friendly Troops/Non-Combatants. Urban operations increase the potential for weapons employment close to friendly forces or non-combatants. Weapons delivery in these situations must attempt to eliminate the possibility of fratricide and minimize collateral damage.

h. Munitions Classes. Table IV-7 provides a listing of classes of munitions that may be considered for use on urban terrain.

Table IV-7. Munitions and Delivery Techniques

Method	Munitions					
	GP	Rocket	Gun	MAV	LGB Self	LGB Assisted
Level	X	X	X	X	X	X
Dive	X	X	X	X	X	X
Pop	X	X	X	X	X	X
Toss	X					
Loft	X	X			X	X

i. Advantages/Disadvantages.

(1) Each of the munitions and delivery techniques has unique advantages and disadvantages. Table IV-8 outlines some advantages and disadvantages of selected munitions and the various delivery techniques associated with fixed-wing aircraft.

Table IV-8. Munitions Advantages and Disadvantages

Type Munitions	Advantage	Disadvantage
General Purpose Bombs	Multi-Service common, Selectable fuzing options Multi-target effective Varying weapons effects Good standoff	Non-precision
Rockets	Multi-Service common Light armor effective Varying weapons effects Good marking device	Non-precision Decreased standoff Increased aircrew exposure
20mm/30mm Cannon	Multi-Service common Light armor effective (20mm cannon) All armor effective (30mm cannon)	Decreased standoff Increased aircrew exposure
Maverick Missiles	Multi-Service common Increased standoff Precision capability Mobile target effective	Decreased effectiveness in adverse weather and non-optimal atmospheric conditions
Laser Guided Bombs	Increased standoff Precision capability Multi-target effective Mobile target effective	Decreased effectiveness in adverse weather and non-optimal atmospheric conditions Requires guidance post release
JDAM	Multi-Service common Selectable fuzing options Multi-target effective All weather capable Accurate Good standoff	Not compatible for moving targets Requires precise target coordinates
JSOW / AGM-154	Multi-service common Selectable fuzing options Multi-target effective All weather capable Accurate Good standoff	Compatible for some moving targets Requires precise target coordinates

(2) The advantages and disadvantages associated with fixed-wing delivery methods and techniques are listed in Table IV-9.

Table IV-9. Delivery Methods Advantages and Disadvantages

Delivery Method	Advantages	Disadvantages
Level	Increased Standoff	Decreased Accuracy (Non-PGM)
Dive	Good Standoff (Medium to High Altitude) Increasingly Accurate Computed Deliveries Highly Accurate (PGM)	Axis Restrictive
Pop	Decreased Long to Medium Range Threat Acquisition & Targeting Time	Increased exposure to target area threat arrays Minimal target tracking time Axis restrictive
Toss	Good Standoff Decreased aircrew exposure	Decreased accuracy Axis restrictive
Loft	Excellent Standoff	Decreased accuracy (Non-PGM)

(3) Buddy lasing of laser-guided bombs (LGB) can be executed from several axes that are dictated by the designator (air or ground). A list of profiles with associated advantages and disadvantages is in Table IV-10.

Table IV-10. Airborne and Ground Designators Advantages and Disadvantages

Type Designator	Advantages	Disadvantages
Airborne:	Increased Standoff Larger target area footprint	Larger laser spot size Increased susceptibility to podium effect
1. Trail Position	Increased probability of success (spot detection) Increased standoff	Axis restrictive Increased platform predictability
2. Overhead Wheel Position	Decreased platform predictability Good standoff	Decreased effectiveness in target areas with varying vertical developments (podium effect)
3. Offset or Opposing Wheel Position	Decreased platform predictability Excellent Standoff	Axis Restrictive Increased susceptibility to podium effect, coordination intensive
Ground	Smaller laser spot size Decreased targeting ambiguity Rapid battle damage assessment (BDA)	Axis restrictive Increased designator exposure Coordination intensive

Appendix A
AIR MISSION PLANNING GUIDELINES

The following items are areas to review during mission planning. While these topics may be common, they have increased applicability to aviation urban operations.

1. Mission Analysis

a. Determine restrictions and constraints.

b. Determine number of aircraft required to accomplish mission (minimize, if possible).

c. Update information before takeoff, en route, and as often as necessary during the mission (urban air operations can become very fluid).

2. Conduct Risk Assessment and Management

3. Friendly Situation

a. Obtain current information regarding friendly forces.

b. Analyze the concept of operations.

4. Threat

a. Know enemy capabilities and limitations.

b. Review known enemy positions.

5. Terrain Analysis

a. Perform flight hazards assessment, physical and environmental.

b. Determine dominant terrain/structures.

c. Determine surface mobility, above ground, street level, and subterranean.

d. Determine degree of terrain relief and variations in building height.

6. Weather

a. Evaluate weather and illumination data.

b. Evaluate enemy's weather capabilities.

7. Route Planning and Navigation

a. Plan ingress, egress, and contingency routes to minimize the duration of flight over urban terrain.

b. Use alternate flight routes, be unpredictable. (Urban operations tend to overuse routes)

8. Terminal Area Procedures

a. Plan terminal area actions in detail (airfields, HLZs, PZs, DZs, etc.).

b. Determine the effects of weather (urban specific) and enemy positions.

9. Communications

a. Determine communications limitations between aircrew and ground forces.

b. Include visual signals.

c. Create a solid alternate communications plan.

10. Airspace Control

a. Know the controlling agencies and required procedures.

b. Request additional measures as required.

11. Rules of Engagement

a. Ensure identification, friend, or foe (IFF) and aircraft survivability equipment (ASE) is working.

b. Understand the purpose and demarcation lines for IFF and ASE. (more complicated in urban operations)

12. Weapons Selection and Employment

a. Clearly mark and confirm targets; know forbidden targets.

b. Ensure a common reference system is used.

13. Contingencies

Develop plans for casualties, personnel recovery (PR) (Appendix D), communications, navigation, weapons, and aircraft systems.

Appendix B

JOINT INTELLIGENCE PREPARATION OF THE BATTLESPACE

1. Process

a. The JIPB process assists in planning aviation urban operations. The process in JP 2-01.3, *JTTP for Joint Intelligence Preparation of the Battlespace*, 2nd Draft, 1 Feb 98, is used to produce intelligence assessments, estimates, and other intelligence products supporting decision making process. All forces must have a thorough understanding of the process.

b. The varied nature of the threats in urban operations requires liaison with local police, militia, NGO, etc., to acquire the information needed for JIPB and mission planning. JIPB is a continuous process involving four major steps:

(1) Defining the total battlespace environment,

(2) Describing the battlespace's effects,

(3) Evaluating the adversary,

(4) Determining and describing the adversary's potential courses of action (COA), most likely COA, and the COA most dangerous to friendly forces and mission accomplishment.

c. The JIPB process is used to analyze the environment and determine an adversary's capabilities to operate within it. JIPB products are used by staffs to prepare their estimates. They are applied during the analysis and selection of a friendly COA. The size and location of the battlespace, objectives, avenues of approach, effects of weather and terrain, and the COA of adversary forces are some of the areas of information required for urban operations addressed in this process. Initial JIPB for aviation must orient aircrews for operations in cluttered urban terrain. The type of urban terrain, the availability of information and collection sources, and the type of operations being conducted affect the amount of information on threat forces of significant military factors in an urban area. Urban operations may require greater use of information derived from HUMINT. The JIPB process should provide aircrews imagery and target overlays facilitating all mission types. Aircrews must carefully review applicable products ensuring they satisfy mission requirements. Further information on the intelligence preparation of the battlespace (IPB) process is found in the following:

(1) FM 34-130, Intelligence Preparation of the Battlefield.

(2) White Paper, Air Force Preparation of the Battlespace, 16 Feb 99.

d. A thorough JIPB process including a map and photoreconnaissance review prepares aircrews before mission execution. Upon mission receipt, aircrews should request the necessary maps and intelligence products. Aerial imagery is an invaluable tool providing clear terrain visualization. It is preferable, although not always possible, to have imagery from the same aspect flown by the aircraft.

2. Resources and Products

a. Validated geospatial products should be used to ensure a common operating picture. Regardless of the geospatial product used, you must use a common reference and marking system. The products must be well prepared, provide clarity, and be available to the aircrews. Intelligence cells should be assisted by at least one operational aviator to ensure production of useful products.

b. Information regarding urban terrain is available from non-military sources. Units must be proactive in gathering of civilian maps, tourist information, cultural information, etc., from other sources. Preliminary JIPB can begin based on open-source information used in conjunction with the excellent variety of intelligence products prepared by Department of Defense (DOD) agencies. Developing a working relationship with potential sources of information and an understanding of the request process improves potential access to some of these products. (Table B-1) Familiarity with the products available allows the unit intelligence sections to request them in the early planning stages.

Table B-1. General Sources

PRODUCT	SOURCES		Civilian/Open		Military/Intelligence
Urban Area Overview	A,B,C,D,E,G,1,2	A	Almanac or Atlas	1	Country Study
UTFO	B,C,2,3	B	Tourist Information	2	Aeronautical Charts
UTOG	B,C,4,5,7	C	Tourist Maps	3	DOD FLIP
FHM	2,3,5,9	D	Civ. Media (print)	4	NIMA Tactical Maps
Threat Analysis	D,E,F,1,5,7	E	Civ. Media (broadcast)	5	Imagery
Target/Objective Catalog	B,C,D,E,I,5,6,7,9	F	Interview	6	Direct Reconnaissance
MCOO	B,C,4,5,6,7,8	G	InterNet Sites	7	S2/G2/J2 RFI
Roof Cover Overlay	5,7	H	Defense Publications	8	G5 Civil Affairs
		I	City Files (local gov't)	9	DIA Products & Pubs

c. Gridded Reference Graphic (GRG). Prepared by the Defense Intelligence Agency (DIA), this large format imagery product (17" X 21") provides an overview map, a small-scale imagery mosaic, and large-scale individual prints of a specific target area. The GRG is typically focused on urban areas but are also produced to cover large maneuver areas and LOCs. The GRG compliments NIMA city graphics (1:12,500 scale) and provides excellent detail for urban mission planning.

d. Contingency Support Study (CSS). Prepared by DIA the CSS has a large format imagery product (17" X 21"). It is designed to support planning for theater operations and contingency planning. Text information includes weather and climate data, oceanography and landing beaches (amphibious operations), terrain analysis, and significant facilities. An overview map and a large-scale map of the target area(s) are included. The CSS is typically focused on an urban area, military facility, or significant terrain. It includes high-resolution electro-optical (EO) and land satellite (LANDSAT) imagery.

e. Contingency Support Package (CSP). Prepared by DIA, the CSP is a large format (17" X 21") and small format (8" X 13") imagery product. It is produced in response to a specific crisis. The CSP is a mission-oriented product, typically supporting NEO. Imagery includes embassy, the ambassador's residence, evacuation routes, AA, HLZ, beaches, ports, and airfields. The format is similar to that of the CSS. High-resolution imagery supports the Section 1500 Department of State (DOS) emergency action plan (EAP).

f. NEO Packet (NEOPAC). Prepared by NIMA, it contains maps, imagery, and information from the Section 1500 DOS EAP for a country. The NEOPAC includes a tactical pilotage chart (TPC) (1:500,000), a Joint operations graphics (JOG) (A)(1:250,000), a tactical land map (TLM) (1:50,000), and a city graphic (1:12,500). Some packets include a lithographic quality image annotated with key routes, terrain, and facilities.

g. NISH. Prepared by the unified commands to support NEO planning, it is coordinated with Section 1500 DOS EAP. Contents include small format imagery (8" X 11") and a text product. The NISH includes overhead imagery of ports, airfields, HLZ, potential evacuation routes, and beaches. Photography and diagrams of pertinent US government facilities.

h. DOS Report. Prepared on an irregular basis, this report includes data on US citizens registered with the local embassy. The report may include available data on tourists, contractors, missionaries, humanitarian workers, US government employees, Marine security guards, diplomatic and defense attaché personnel, military advisors, and government dependents. It may also include data on foreign personnel to be evacuated.

i. Safe area intelligence description (SAID). Prepared by DIA, the SAID includes foldout imagery and text data in support of survival, evasion, recovery, and escape (SERE) planning. It includes small-scale EO imagery, an orientation map, and climate, terrain and weather data. When available, contact and extraction points are described and annotated on maps and imagery. The SAID covers designated geographical regions.

j. Marine air-ground task force (MAGTF) SERE Plan (USMC). Prepared by Marine Expeditionary Unit (MEU) S-2, this product usually includes a local counterintelligence assessment, civilian attitudes toward American forces, ethnic or tribal affiliations, recent unrest or violence, active paramilitary or terrorist groups, and language and religious demographics. Evasion and extraction data includes central orientation point(s) for SERE, signaling methods, radio frequencies, pickup times, primary and alternate extraction sites/HLZ. Survival data includes indigenous plants, animals, terrain analysis, and local weather trends. Imagery includes expected target areas and potential extraction sites.

k. Tactical recovery of aircraft & personnel (TRAP) orientation package (USMC). The MEU S-2 prepares this package in coordination with MEU S-3 based on the mission requirements. It includes maps and imagery to facilitate rapid reaction to downed aircraft. All materials applicable to the operational area are prepackaged for rapid orientation of the recovery and security elements.

l. Joint annual review of SERE production (JARSP). Prepared by the Joint Services SERE Agency (JSSA). The JARSP lists blood chits, evasion charts designated SAFE area products, and SERE after action reports from past operations. The JARSP details the procedure for ordering the listed SERE products.

m. Psychological operations (PSYOP) studies. These are prepared by the US Army 4th Psychological Operations Group, strategic studies detachments (SSD) and the National Ground Intelligence Center (NGIC). There are four types of PSYOP studies: the PSYOP Annex to Military Capabilities Study (MCS), the Basic PSYOP Study (BPS), the Special PSYOP Study (SPS), and the Special PSYOP Assessment (SPA). The MCS summarizes PSYOP relevant issues. The BPS is a nine-chapter document that analyzes the PSYOP environment and vulnerabilities of selected countries to include political, economic, and cultural characteristics. The SPS is formatted like the BPS but has a narrower focus. It addresses such subjects as specific target groups, regional or geographical areas, social institutions, and media analysis. Perceptions towards the US or issues important to specific population groups may also be discussed. The SPA is a time sensitive intelligence memorandum (usually an electronic message) providing assessments of significant crisis situations, events, or issues from a PSYOP standpoint. Requests for any of the four PYSOP studies are made through PSYOP or SOF units or staff liaison elements supporting the JFC. Studies are also available from the intelligence link (INTELINK) of the Special Operations Command Research, Analysis, and Threat Evaluation System (SOCRATES).

n. Basic Targeting Graphic (BTG). The BTG is prepared in support of theater operations or contingency plans. It is updated regularly (3-4 year intervals) in support of an operations plan (OPLAN). The BTG includes 11" X 16" format high-resolution EO imagery. It also includes an orientation map, small-scale orientation photo(s), and annotated large-scale imagery. The focus of most BTGs is military and industrial targets in urban areas.

o. Intelligence Support Package (ISP). Prepared by DIA, the product includes graphics, LANDSAT and LANDSAT-digital terrain evaluation data (DTED) merge imagery, maps, target line drawings, photography (when available), and multi-scale EO imagery. A target summary provides data on target significance, description, imagery annotations, node functions, air defenses, and critical nodal analysis. The ISP is produced in response to the theater or joint task force (JTF) target list or a request for information (RFI). The ISP supports targeting of specific military and civilian installations.

p. Critical elements of selected generic installations. Previously published by DIA, the product includes imagery and text discussion of general categories of man-made structures and facilities. They describe functional components and critical nodes of military, industrial, and transportation facilities. The also assess damage and repair time of key components.

q. Digital terrain analysis mapping system (DTAMS). The DTAMS facilitates the production and updating of maps. It also allows creation of detailed drawings of urban areas and large-scale diagrams of specific targets, objectives, and HLZs. DTAMS is capable of generating grid overlay of objective areas for fire support, etc. New maps can be produced in three to four hours. Old maps may be updated within two hours.

r. Video support product (VSP). Produced by the Marine Corps Intelligence Activity (MCIA), the VSP is an annotated and narrated video home system (VHS) videotape of EO imagery. It is oriented towards a specific mission.

s. Top Scene. The Naval Strike Warfare Center (NSWC) at Naval Air Station (NAS) Fallon, Nevada produces Top Scene. Top Scene includes a VHS tape product, merging EO imagery with DTED. It provides oblique and vertical coverage at various altitudes and ranges from the target or objective. It is oriented towards naval air strike mission planning.

t. Pattern Analysis. Prepared by USMC MEU S-2, this product includes multiple map overlays and text assessing military or terrorist activity in an urban area.

u. TerraBase II. Terrabase II is a terrain evaluation tool for the exploitation of readily available NIMA standard gridded and raster products. The system works on a Windows 95 or Windows NT operating system. It produces LOS, weapons fans/visible area plots (VAP), oblique, perspective, and elevation views, elevation tints, contour plots, slope tints, reflective plots, point elevations, range circles, fly-through/terrain walk tactical decision aids and more.

v. Digital Topographic Support System (DTSS). This US Army system provides commanders a means of producing a variety of topographic products using terrain models. The system has the capability to produce multiple, full-color, hard copy terrain products.

w. Urban Terrain Feature Overlay (UTFO)–Vertical & Lateral References. This product is used to prepare aircrews for aviation urban operations. It annotates prominent navigation features as points (vertical structures), lines (lateral references), or areas. The altitude in feet mean sea level (MSL) and, in parenthesis, height AGL, i.e., "1460' (940'), follows vertical features. Elevation data, both MSL and AGL, is important for mission planning. This overlay may be combined with the urban terrain orientation graphic (UTOG) detailed below. The UTFO identifies and plots:

(1) Dominant vertical features,

(2) Significant linear features,

(3) Prominent, unique structures,

(4) Currently known deliberate hazards or helicopter countermeasures.

x. UTOG. (Figure B-1) This product is used for aircrew orientation. A graphical depiction of urban terrain characteristics allows a more thorough orientation than map reconnaissance alone. The UTOG is prepared by dividing the terrain into areas classified by density of structures and building construction. Digital Feature Analysis Data (DFAD) codes may be used on overlay products to minimize clutter. This product serves as a substitute for the traditional combined obstacle overlay (COO) for aviation operations and may be combined with the UTFO. The UTOG lends itself for use by the S-3 and fire support element (FSE) for development of the battle tracking overlay (BTO). The UTOG provides the following urban area general characteristics:

(1) Density of structures,

(2) Building Construction,

(3) Street pattern.

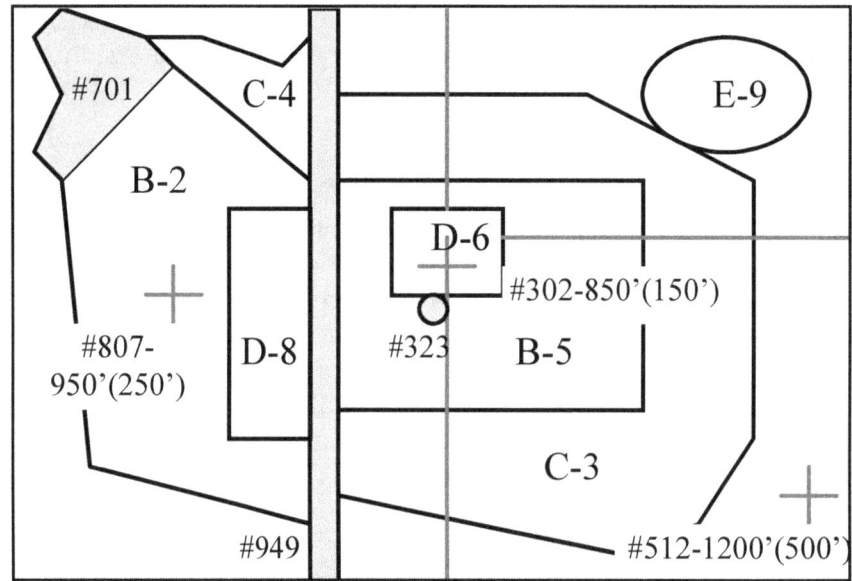

Figure B-1. Combined UTOG/UTF Overlay (Simplified Example)

y. Target/Objective (T/O) Catalog. The T/O Catalog is a technical database of urban facilities and structures. It is essentially a record of data collected for features throughout the operational area. The DFAD numbering system may be used for identification of prominent reference features and for development of a T/O catalog. This allows computerized search and rapid access to T/O data based on location, DFAD feature identification (FID) code, or other characteristics. Priority should be placed on features of navigational significance, followed by other structures based on importance. Building and continuously updating a T/O catalog allows rapid and effective mission planning.

z. Modified Combined Obstacle Overlay (MCOO). The urban MCOO usually reflects terrain effects on ground maneuver. It combines trafficability data found on a COO with avenues of approach, friendly situation, enemy situation, and potential enemy objectives. Additional urban terrain factors that influence the ground tactical situation are underground systems that provide concealed mobility corridors. These can be annotated on a separate overlay.

aa. Avenues of Approach Overlay. The overlay considers unique terrain effects and obstacles, such as urban damage and rubble. This product may be unnecessary if a MCOO has been prepared.

bb. Roof Coverage Overlay. In urban terrain, roof coverage is more meaningful to aviation operations than a ground-based horizontal visibility (fields of fire) analysis. This overlay depicts concealment from aerial observation and directly relates to the density of structures. (Figure B-2)

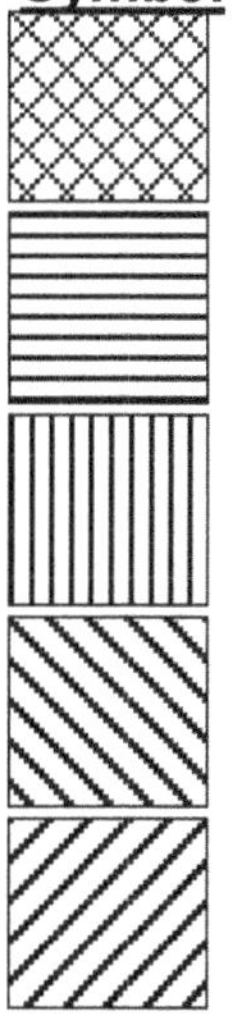

Symbol	% Roof	Category	Concealment
	75-100	Congested	Excellent
	50-75	Dense	Good
	25-50	Moderate	Fair
	5-25	Sparse	Poor
	0-5	Open	None

Figure B-2. Roof Coverage

cc. Threat Evaluation. This analysis is prepared based on the enemy situation and doctrine. An overlay depicts possible and likely enemy COA.

3. Imagery

a. Imagery is an excellent way of obtaining detailed information about potential objective areas. There are several considerations to observe when using imagery: resolution, specific requirements, and date. The resolution must be sufficient to provide the type of specific information required. The resolution of overhead national technical means (NTM) EO imagery is measured by the national imagery interpretability rating scale (NIIRS) and is divided into 10 rating levels. The NIIRS is based on the ability to *detect, distinguish between,* and *identify* objects and structures on the image. For example, a NIIRS 1 image allows you to detect or distinguish between taxiways and runways at a large airfield. NIIRS 5 allows identification of small items such as individual rail cars.

An NIIRS 6 image can identify automobiles as sedans or station wagons. A NIIRS 9 product should detect individual spikes holding railroad track. As a general rule, NIIRS 5 to 7 images are of sufficient resolution to provide staffs and aircrews sufficient detail needed for planning operations. For SOF or SAR missions, imagery with greater resolution may be required.

b. Requests for current, high-resolution imagery may require a significant time to fulfill. Avoid over-tapping limited resources and assets by asking only for what you need. Consult the NIIRS manual or your intelligence unit for more information about imagery products.

c. Specify information requirements precisely. If you are executing a pre-planned SAR mission or expect to ingress/egress a city from a certain direction at a specific time, request imagery that closely resembles that profile. The lead-time for obtaining imagery to meet specific requirements are based on prioritization of needs and may entail a time lag between the time of the request to dissemination of the product. The characteristics of various imaging techniques and the peculiarities of various imaging platforms should be thoroughly understood to maximize the use of the information. For example, imagery taken at an oblique angle versus straight overhead aids in determining heights of building and obstacles. It also helps highlight utility poles. Early coordination with intelligence sections assists in obtaining data from national, theater, and tactical assets.

d. There are vast amounts of archived imagery available. If older imagery meets operational requirements, it may be more quickly obtained than newly generated requests for imagery. It is important to carefully evaluate the risks of using dated information. For example, in Operation RESTORE DEMOCRACY, a unit planned flight routes in Port-au-Prince using overhead imagery. The ingress route followed a canal, and the aircrew plan to use identifiable bridges as navigation aids to find a specific street. Unfortunately, the photos were over a year old and depicted three bridges over the canal. The unit discovered one of the bridges was no longer there. This caused momentary confusion overcome by reference to other terrain features based on their imagery study.

e. In addition to image resolution and currency of the information, there is a variety of imagery products available. These include three-dimensional imagery of the T/O area, obtainable in different scales, that is useful for determining the height relationship of buildings in the objective area. Large wall-sized imagery sheets are available and can be used for planning, briefing, intelligence updates, and updating hazards. Whenever possible, compare the most current imagery available to map products to ensure the most current and accurate data are used for mission planning and execution.

Appendix C
MUNITIONS

1. Laser-Guided Bomb

a. LGBs offer accurate targeting using laser terminal guidance. Various weapons yields are available based on Mark 82, 83, or 84 series weapons. Paveway II guidance kits attached to the appropriate series weapons make up the guided bomb unit (GBU). Urban LGB considerations include building proximity, laser LOS, podium effects due to building faces, collateral damage due to weapon yield, guidance failure, smoke, haze, and rubble.

b. Planners should use the JMEM to determine weapons effects associated with the appropriate GBU. In general LGBs provide good capability against soft targets due to the associated blast, fragmentation, and overpressure. Penetration capability is enhanced with delayed fusing and increased impact angles. Use Bomb Live Unit (BLU) 109 bomb bodies against hard targets when desiring deep weapon penetration. Weapons impact angles are generally determined based on horizontal targets. The weapon impact angle against vertical targets can be estimated by adding approximately 90 degrees to the horizontal impact angle.

c. Laser spot placement should be considered due to the tendency for GBU weapons to impact short of a target. Laser designators should elevate the laser spot relative to the desired impact point to offset inherent trajectory sag associated with LGBs. Elevating the laser spot allows the GBU to maintain a higher potential energy level into the terminal phase of the flight at which time the spot can be shifted down and onto the desired impact point.

2. Maverick (AGM-65 Block B/D/E/G/K)

a. AGM-65 Maverick provides a launch and leave precision guided munitions capability in urban terrain operations. AGM-65 A/B models are centroid tracking EO versions which utilize a shaped charge warhead and are capable against small, point targets such as vehicles, including armor. AGM-65 D is similar, except it uses IR imaging to track targets. Larger targets may be engaged using the AGM-65 G, or an IR Maverick with a HE warhead. The G model Maverick has a forced correlation capability. This allows selection of a specific desired mean point of impact (DMPI) on larger targets as well as a ground selectable fuzing delay allowing the missile to penetrate the outer surface of the target and detonate inside. AGM-65K utilizes an EO seeker, carries the same blast warhead as the AGM-65G, and provides significantly greater standoff range than the AGM-65B. It also has forced correlation track capability. Time of flight of the missile should be considered when employing the AGM-65 against moving vehicle targets in urban terrain since terrain masking due to vertical obstructions will cause the missile to break lock. Once the missile breaks lock, its flight path will become unpredictable, but it remains armed and will detonate upon impact. Consideration should be given to releasing at closer slant ranges if friendly forces are in close proximity to the target to minimize the missile time of flight. When using the AGM-65 G in the force correlation mode, consideration should be given to the apparent target size when engaging targets in close proximity to friendly positions. A decrease in slant range will provide a larger apparent target, which in turn will allow a more precise aimpoint to be selected.

b. For the AGM-65F IR Maverick, breaklock algorithms will cause the missile to go into a correlate track or "stare" mode. In this mode, the weapon will attempt to track any object closest to the centroid of the IR scene at breaklock. If this occurs, there is no guarantee that it is the intended target. If no other object is present, the missile will drive to the centroid of the IR scene and detonate. The hit will be entirely dependent on the composition of the missile's IR scene. The point of impact relative to the intended target can only be a guess.

c. Regarding the AGM-65E Laser Maverick, if the proper laser source is lost for over 1.5 seconds the missile will safe itself and assume a lofted profile. The intent is for the missile to land long as a dud. This feature, in addition to the modest yield and excellent penetration characteristics make it a potential weapon for urban CAS.

3. Cluster Munitions

a. Generally, cluster munitions are appropriate for use in the urban environment only in very limited circumstances. The area effects of the weapon and relatively high dud rate of the submunitions often make them inappropriate for use in densely populated areas because of their great potential for immediate and persistent civilian collateral damage. If specific circumstances suggest the use of cluster munitions, very careful consideration should be given to the collateral damage likely to result. Particularly after air operations in Kosovo, the use of air delivered cluster munitions has become a very sensitive one in the international community. Expect that approval authority for the use of cluster munitions will be retained at higher levels in future operations.

b. Cluster Bomb Units (CBU) include mark (Mk) -20 Rockeye, CBU-87 combined effects munition (CEM), CBU-89 Gator air delivered mines, and CBU-97 sensor-fuzed weapon (SFW). Each weapon uses a dispenser. Rockeye uses a shaped charge penetrator and is typically used against armor. CEM bomblets have three kill mechanisms, shaped-charge penetration, fragmentation, and incendiary. The Gator consists of anti-armor and antipersonnel mines. SFWs consists of submunitions designed for use against tanks, armored vehicles, artillery, armored personnel carriers (APC), and support vehicles.

c. Cluster weapons can be equipped with either a mechanical time fuze or radar proximity fuze. The type of fuze will dictate the type of delivery option/ mode to use.

(1) While very reliable, time fuzes do not allow a great deal of flexibility in delivery options. Once the arming time is selected prior to flight, it cannot be changed. When unsure whether a low-altitude or medium-altitude employment

option will be used during the mission, set the primary time for a medium-altitude option and the option time for a low-altitude option.

(2) Proximity fuzes provide greater flexibility for delivery of the cluster weapon. Variations in munitions time of fall will not affect the fuze function altitude as long as fuze-arming restrictions are met. Delivery parameters can be adjusted for the situation.

d. Advantages of CBU over general-purpose bombs include:

(1) good area coverage,

(2) very effective against personnel and soft-skinned vehicles ,

(3) ability to penetrate armor,

(4) low-altitude deliveries.

e. CBU-89 provides a minefield for a controlled period and is excellent for a denial/channelization

f. Disadvantages of CBU include:

(1) fixed employment slant ranges for timed fuzes,

(2) high drag,

(3) dud bomblets,

(4) time-delay bomblets may hinder friendly passage through an area,

(5) pattern size and coverage make delivery in a troops in contact (TIC) situation difficult, if not impossible.

4. Joint Direct Attack Munition (JDAM) (GBU-29, GBU-30, GBU-31, GBU-32)

a. The JDAM can be used for CAS, interdiction, SEAD, naval anti-surface warfare, and amphibious strike missions. This munition serves to upgrade the existing inventory of Mk 80 series general-purpose bombs. This is accomplished by integrating it with an INS/GPS guidance kit. JDAM variants for the Mk-81 250-pound and Mk-82 500-pound bombs are designated GBU-29 and GBU-30, respectively. The Mk-83 1,000-pound, and Mk-84 2,000-pound general-purpose bombs, are designated as the GBU-31 and GBU-32. Hard Target penetrators that are being changed into low-cost JDAM include the 2,000-pound BLU-109 and 1,000-pound BLU-110.

b. The JDAM can be continuously updated by aircraft avionics systems before release. Once released, the INS/GPS of the bomb will take over and guide the bomb to its target regardless of weather. Guidance is accomplished via the tight coupling of an accurate GPS with a 3-axis INS. The guidance control unit provides accurate guidance in both GPS-aided INS modes of operation and INS-only modes of operation. This inherent JDAM capability will counter the threat from near-term technological advances in GPS jamming. The weapon system allows launch from very low to very high altitude. It can also be launched in a dive, toss, loft, or in straight and level flight with an on-axis or off-axis delivery. JDAM also allows multiple target engagements on a single pass delivery. JDAM provides the user with a variety of targeting schemes, such as preplanned and in-flight captive carriage retargeting.

5. Tube launched, Optically tracked, Wire guided (TOW)

a. The TOW is a precision guided munition (PGM) with a small CEP. The minimum engagement range is 500 meters. An external guidance mechanism (laser) is not required. The warhead is able to penetrate urban structures as well as conventional armor.

b. The following discussion concerning the "Hellfire" covers PGM and shaped charge characteristics in detail, however the TOW delivery mechanics are mentioned here as the guidance mechanisms differ. When using TOW in an urban environment, building types will have to be analyzed to determine window locations, type construction (framed or frameless), etc. Generally, framed buildings are newer and use steel girder construction; Therefore, it will be harder to achieve the desired effects with a shaped charge warhead than when used against frameless building, which tends to be an older masonry structure. The structure construction will determine whether the building's room is destroyed, the building collapses, or the target is unharmed. Generally, TOW missiles are not fired into an open window or aperture because the PGM warhead will travel through the room and impact the other side of the room and far wall. This will negate the warhead effects since the warhead will detonate and explode into the wrong room. Depending on the building, target, and desired effects, TOWs may be aimed at windows, the upper, middle, or lower one-third part of a building side, or into the roof.

6. Hellfire

a. Shaped charged warheads are not optimized against urban structures. TOW or Hellfire can destroy small buildings constructed of light wood, metal, or concrete. TOW or Hellfire shaped charge penetration of generic (brick, concrete, or wood) building structures will generally be limited to one compartment of the building due to shaped charge size, shaped charge impact characteristics, and average missile velocity. As a rule of thumb, Hellfire shaped charge jet penetration is 42 inches of rolled homogenous armor (RHA), 10.5 feet of non-reinforced concrete, 12 feet of wood, and 12.5 feet of unconfined sand. In general, expect a TOW warhead to blow an 8-18 inch hole in 8 inches of double reinforced concrete and a 5-12 inch hole in triple brick. Firing a TOW into cinder block blows a 3-5 foot hole, or roughly large enough for a man to crawl through. The size is not only dependent on the material, but also on the angle of attack upon impact. A higher angle of impact against a vertical surface increases the net effective thickness of the wall that the warhead must travel through (similar to sloped armor). Expect the missile body, motor, and casing to travel into the room, adding to the spalling effect. With more porous materials (concrete), the spalling fragments are larger, but they lose energy quicker and do not travel as far into the room. The resulting cloud of masonry dust is an ineffective kill mechanism, but has the equivalent effect of throwing sand into someone's eyes. The dust cloud covers an approximately ten foot square area. Against masonry structures, masonry dust will affect personnel inside the room and dust will be visible coming from the impact hole.

b. Shaped charge warheads can penetrate the above materials. Localized spalling normally spreads out from the entry point in an approximate 6-inch to 1-foot spall cone. The warhead effect immediately starts to breakup inside the building, but due to its speed, may travel some distance before stopping. When impacting an outer wall (reinforced concrete or triple brick), most of the overpressure is dissipated outside of the building upon impact. The following peak overpressure effects are achievable with the Hellfire shaped charge warhead: 3 pounds per square inch (psi) at 60 feet, 6 psi at @ 40 feet, and 12 psi at 25 feet. A rule of thumb for comparing any warhead penetration against 6500 psi concrete is: steel thickness divided by .556 equals the equivalent 6500 psi concrete penetration. Example: 2 inches of steel/.556 = 3.6 inches of concrete equivalent. Therefore, knowing what a warhead can penetrate in terms of steel allows a conservative estimate of concrete penetration. It is important to note, though, that concrete density and building materials vary across the world. Shaped charged warheads will still penetrate any building material, but the internal effect may be lessened. The overpressure falls off quickly and is equivalent to the cube of the radius from the impact. For comparison - if a nominal warhead could produce lethal effects against personnel at 2 feet, then at 8 feet the effects would render personnel unconscious, and at 512 feet, the effects would be heard, but not felt. The incidental overpressure effects are of a very short duration (<30 milliseconds) and may not cause immediate incapacitation, but require several minutes before internal bodily effects are felt on such organs as the kidney, liver, spleen, eardrums, etc. If the material is thin, the missile will pass through the material and expend most of its overpressure inside the building upon impact with the interior wall/floor. Only 1 inch plywood, or equivalent, is required to detonate the Hellfire warhead. If the warhead is shot through an aperture (ex. window glass, doorway, etc.), the resulting overpressure will be much greater inside the building or room. However, the incapacitative spalling is lessened because the warhead travels through the room and impacts on the back wall of the room. At short distances (room width) the spalling cone has not had time to expand, therefore only enemy personnel directly within the spall cone will be injured by the spall. However, total kill mechanisms include heat, flash blindness, eardrum rupture, concussion, and fragments. Shaped charged warheads are not optimized against urban structures, however, shooting a missile into a building or room should immobilize the enemy, if not kill him. A moderate Pi (*fragmentary effects only*) is achievable with a TOW or Hellfire used against double reinforced concrete or triple brick.

c. Against a 10-inch thick, non-reinforced concrete structure, Hellfire normally produces a clear hole approximately 3 feet in diameter. Two missiles fired in rapid or ripple can be very effective against reinforced concrete structures. The first missile clears an approximate 3 foot opening that fills with smoke for several seconds. The second missile is guided through the opening creating significantly greater overpressure inside. Any remaining reinforcement bars should cause the second missile to detonate on the wall, reducing the effect, although overpressure inside the enclosure rises markedly at detonation because of the large opening. Highly volatile materials inside the enclosure may produce too much smoke from the first missile, creating a tracking hazard for the second missile and affecting accuracy.

d. Actual measured data in a bunker indicates that the spall shower can be a very effective secondary weapon given a masonry or armored steel target. In a test firing, the warhead detonated 4 feet in front of the bunker in earth terrain before penetrating 30 inches of reinforced concrete bunker wall. Overpressure and concrete spall destroyed two anthropomorphic dummies inside the bunker. The spall shower had a weight of 128 pounds and lethal concrete fragments were recovered from witness panels at a density of over 12 fragments per square foot on the back of the 20 square foot bunker. The jet passed through the 12 inch reinforced concrete rear wall and greater than 3 feet into the surrounding earth embankment. Typical brick or masonry structures will react similar to the bunker but thinner walls will produce proportionally smaller spall showers.

e. The tandem warhead is not expected to make any difference in the effect on occupants inside the building relative to a single high explosive anti-tank (HEAT) warhead, regardless of whether the warhead detonates inside or outside. During Operation Just Cause in Panama, one missile was fired into each floor of a headquarters building. Although the missiles detonated upon contact with the windows, internal blast overpressure gutted an entire floor overturning furniture and file cabinets and igniting combustibles.

f. The amount of overpressure inside confined spaces depends upon the internal volume of the enclosure. It is also modified by the volume of solids in the enclosure, such as furniture, file cabinets, and personnel.

g. The Hellfire is not a quick reaction CAS weapon. To employ Hellfire in an urban environment requires careful consideration of LOS geometry. Hellfire provides standoff capability versus enemy air defense at the expense of increasing altitude to obtain LOS. If using autonomous designating, a balance between designator LOS and exposure to the enemy weapons engagement zone (WEZ) is required. The Hellfire trajectory is optimized for an up and over, top-down attack profile in order to defeat enemy tanks. The trajectory ranges from 10 to 25 degrees downward at impact. This trajectory can not be changed to fly a direct profile such as the TOW flies. However, this profile is useful in engaging targets in buildings or in streets between buildings. To shape the terminal trajectory to the flattest profile requires understanding the effects of launch mode, range to target, and delay designation. Generally, a flatter profile will be flown at minimum launch ranges, while longer ranges increase the terminal dive angle. Regardless of range or delay, the AGM-114K flies a steeper profile than the AGM-114B. The most significant limitation of PGMs is their minimum arming distance.

7. 20mm Cannon

a. The M56 round will not penetrate heavy armor at tactical ranges. Its penetration on concrete ranges from minimal to none. Precision guidance unit (PGU) rounds will penetrate cinderblock walls and have a reasonable capability versus concrete. On RHA, it penetrates 3/8 inch at 45-degree obliquity at 2500 feet slant range from a 450 knot aircraft. This is approximately equivalent to ½ inch at normal (perpendicular) impact. Vertical surfaces should not dud the M50 series round. High explosive incendiary (HEI) round impacts have the smallest fragmentation pattern and will minimize ricochets, thus minimizing collateral damage. HEI rounds are a potential fire starter when used against wooden structures. Target-practice 20mm rounds ricochet more than HEI rounds. Inert PGU-27 20mm, delivered 7.5 degrees downward, will ricochet as far as the maximum range of the round (2000 meters) and up to 400 feet from the point of impact when delivered against horizontal hard flat surfaces. This ricochet effect may affect noncombatants. HEI rounds (M56A3/A4) can produce casualties to exposed personnel within a +/- 2 meter radius.

b. Tracers are a double-edged weapon in this environment. The normal method of firing 20mm is to shoot, observe the rounds impact, and if necessary, walk the rounds onto the target. However, in urban areas, rounds off target are more likely to cause collateral damage. In Chechnya, the Russians prohibited tracers on any firing platform due to the intense and devastating fire returned from the Chechen rebels. A compromise solution is to mix tracer and non-tracer rounds in a 1:10 mix. Given the M197 rate of fire (650 rounds per minute), a tracer would be seen once for every 10 rounds fired. The reverse is true if the enemy is firing at you with tracer-mixed ammo (i.e., for every tracer seen, 10-20 rounds are never seen). If tracers are not used, 20mm HEI detonations against hard surfaces cue the pilots where the rounds are impacting.

8. 25mm Cannon

a. Both the AC-130U gunship and the AV-8B Harrier use the GAU-12/U 25mm gattling gun.

b. The 25mm cannon is effective against personnel and soft-skinned vehicles in the open or under light cover. It has a maximum capacity of 3,000 rounds and a rate of fire of 1,800 rounds per minute. Burst length is computer adjustable from 15 to 350 rounds. The 25mm cannon is an effective area suppression weapon. Available munitions are HEI, API, and training projectile (TP).

9. 30mm Cannon

a. The M230A1 "Chaingun" is used by the Apache helicopter against soft-skinned and lightly armored targets, and for self-defense. It has a single barrel, externally powered hydraulically driven turret. Maximum capacity is 1200 rounds with a rate of fire of 600-650 rounds per minute. Maximum range is 4,000 meters with a maximum effective range of 1500 to 1700 meters. Ordinance includes the M789 HE dual-purpose ammunition.

b. The GAU-8 30mm cannon is a seven-barrel; percussion primed Gatling gun used by the A-10. It is effective against tanks, armored vehicles, and a variety of mobile and fixed targets. The GAU-8 holds 1,150 rounds and uses three different bullets; TP, HEI, and an armor piercing (AP) depleted uranium round. The AP penetrates armor at slant ranges out to 6,000 feet from a low altitude, less than 15-degree delivery angle and outside 10,000 foot slant range from high dive angles. The HEI round functions at ranges beyond the computed gun sight maximum slant ranges. The TP round is used for training, but possesses a limited penetration capability. The computed gun sight allows accurate employment up to 15,000 foot slant range. The velocity of the GAU-8 bullet 6,000 feet from the muzzle is the same as a 20mm bullet velocity at the muzzle. The high bullet velocity, rate of fire (approximately 70 rounds per second), and small dispersion (5-mile radius for all bullets) provide a good bullet density and a powerful punch. The GAU-8 is a very reliable, accurate, and simple point-and-shoot weapon that can be used close to friendly ground troops and possesses a relatively long-range capability. Disadvantages include a large ricochet pattern, decreased bullet density at shallow dive angles, and long slant ranges.

10. 40mm Cannon

a. The AC-130 Gunship employs the M2A1 Modified 40mm cannon, which fires various types of HE and WP rounds. The 40mm cannon is an effective weapon for urban terrain, especially urban CAS. This weapon is a good compromise between lethality, collateral damage, and fratricide potential. Most 40mm munitions have limited penetration capability. Thus, a significant factor limiting 40mm effectiveness is the abundance of cover for targets in urban terrain. The gun fires a high explosive-plugged (HE-P), high explosive incendiary-plugged (HEI-P), HEI zirconium, and armor piercing tracer (APT) rounds.

b. The HE-P cartridge is used against material and personnel targets. The round utilizes the Mk-27 fuze which functions on light impact. Fuze action time is short, giving the ammunition limited penetration capability. This round is fair against hard targets, but does provide suppression for personnel in the open or under light cover.

c. The HEI-P cartridge is used against material targets. It was developed specifically to increase fire-starting capability against trucks. The round has good incendiary potential but contains less trinitrotoluene (TNT), producing less fragmentation than HE-P. The standard Mk-2 projectile body was modified by adding a metal liner, producing bright sparks on detonation. This effect makes the round a good choice for target marking. In particular, when the gunship cannot maintain constant LOS with the target, a well boresighted system can mark a target even if it cannot observe round impact. Because of the fire-starting potential of this round, carefully consider using it during urban operations.

d. The HEI zirconium cartridge is used against material and personnel targets. It was developed specifically to increase fire-starting capability, while maintaining adequate fragmentation for anti-personnel use. The standard Mk-2 projectile body was completely redesigned by adding additional explosive fill and a zirconium liner, producing bright sparks on impact. Because of the fire-starting potential of this round, carefully consider using it during urban operations.

e. APT rounds penetrate RHA of various thicknesses. The projectile contains no explosives, relying on kinetic energy as its damage mechanism. APT can be used in urban operations to minimize collateral damage. It is generally ineffective against multiple personnel targets and difficult to see the actual impact point of the round.

11. 105mm Cannon

a. The AC-130 Gunship carries an M102 105mm Cannon. This gun fires the 105mm HE rounds.

b. The M102 105mm HE cartridge is used against such targets as personnel, material, and light to medium structures. It has a large lethal fan from shrapnel and blast. Upon detonation, this projectile produces approximately 3,000 fragments. As urban terrain often requires target engagement very near friendly positions, use M102 HE only if adequate cover is available and the target cannot be attacked other means. For other than general-purpose applications, the M102 round can accommodate various fuzes. The M-557 fuze is good for general-purpose point detonation or selectable delayed detonation. It requires a minimum of one inch of wood to function reliably. The M102 performs poorly against hard targets or buildings with thick concrete, brick, or rock walls, unless specifically fuzed for this application. The fused munition unit (FMU)-151/B hardened fuze gives the M102 capability against hard targets in the delay mode. It requires a minimum of two inches of wood to reliably function. The M102 with this fuze will penetrate 10 inches of 5,000 psi reinforced concrete (0 degrees obliquity). When fired against typical structures, the point detonating (PD) function opens holes about three feet in diameter and the delay function results in penetration of exterior walls with detonation immediately inside the wall. For anti-personnel applications, the M-732 fuze detonates the projectile at about 7 meters above the ground. Large buildings in urban terrain may cause the fuze to function early, reducing effectiveness, and increasing collateral damage. The fuze will also point detonate if needed or if the proximity function fails.

12. Rockets

a. 2.75 inch rockets can be used against various urban targets including, light wood frame buildings, personnel, and area targets. The rocket produces a significant psychological impact. Unguided rockets have an inherent dispersion error. Add to this error an aiming error, rocket pod boresight error, and range estimation error, and the results are a larger target dispersion error. Laser rangefinders, launcher stabilization adapters, and firing at close range compensate for some of this dispersion error. Fuze arming may be a factor for short firing range. Mk-423 PD and the Mk-427 PD fuzes arm at 300 feet and 1250 feet respectively. A rule of thumb for the 2.75 inch Mk-151 warhead penetration against 6500 psi concrete is 4 to 6 inches. In addition, smoke, flechette, and visible/IR illumination rounds are available.

b. The 5 inch rocket may be used for dense structures. The Mk-24 Mod 0, M191 warhead and fuze combination penetrates 24 inches of reinforced concrete and becomes armed at 800 feet. However, due to weight restrictions, fewer 5 inch rockets can be carried if a mix of ordnance is desired. The large blast effect, equivalent to 105mm artillery rounds, may not be desired near personnel. For comparison, the Mk-24 general purpose (GP) 5 inch rocket carries approximately 4 times the warhead weight as the 2.75 inch, 1.5 times a TOW, and .7 times the weight of a Hellfire warhead. The 5 inch rocket has similar dispersion error as the 2.75 inch rockets.

13. Medium/heavy Machine-guns (7.62mm and .50 caliber)

a. Machine-guns. The .50-caliber machine-gun and the 7.62-mm M60, M240, and M-134 machine-guns provide high-volume, long-range, automatic fires for suppressing or destroying targets. They can be used to penetrate light structures. The 50-caliber machine-gun is most effective in this role. Tracers from all machine-guns are likely to start fires, but the .50-caliber tracer is more apt to do so.

b. Employment. The primary consideration is the limited availability of long-range fields of fire. Although machine-guns should be employed at the lowest level possible, grazing fire at ground level is often obstructed by rubble. Because of their reduced penetration power, 7.62mm machine-guns are less effective against masonry targets than the .50-caliber. However, their availability and light weight make them well suited to augment heavy machine-guns or in areas where .50-caliber machine-guns cannot be positioned or are not available.

c. Penetration. The range and type of target affects the penetration ability of the 7.62-mm and .50-caliber rounds. At 200 meters, the 7.62-mm ball round penetrates a single layer of sandbags, but not a double layer. The armor-piercing round does only slightly better. Concentrated machine-gun fire penetrates typical wall construction. It will not normally penetrate reinforced concrete structures or dense natural stone walls. Internal walls, partitions, plaster, floors, ceilings, common office furniture, home appliances, and bedding are easily penetrated by both 7.62-mm and .50-caliber rounds. Table C-1 details the penetration characteristics of the 7.62mm ball round.

Table C-1. Penetration Capabilities of 7.62mm (Ball) Round

Range (m)	Pine Boards (in)	Cinder Block (in)	Concrete (in)	Dry Sand (in)
25	13	8	2	5
100	18	10	2	4.5
200	41	8	2	7

d. The .50-caliber round penetrates better at all ranges. For hard targets, obliquity and range affect .50-caliber penetration. Both armor piercing and ball ammunition penetrate 14 inches of sand or 28 inches of packed earth at 200 meters, if the rounds impact perpendicular to the flat face of the target. Table C-2 explains the effect of a 25-degree obliquity on a .50-caliber penetration.

Table C-2. Rounds (Rds) Needed to Penetrate Reinforced Concrete Wall (At a 25-Degree Obliquity)

Thickness (ft)	100 m	200 m
2	300 Rds	1,200 Rds
3	450 Rds	1,800 Rds
4	600 Rds	2,400 Rds

e. Protection. Barriers against small arms are also effective against 7.62-mm rounds with some exceptions. The 7.62-mm round penetrates a windowpane at a 45-degree obliquity, a hollow cinder block, and both sides of a car body. It also penetrates wooden frame buildings. The .50-caliber round penetrates all common urban materials except a sand-filled 55-gallon drum.

Appendix D

PERSONNEL RECOVERY

1. Personnel Recovery

a. PR is an umbrella term for operations focusing on the task of recovering captured, missing, or isolated personnel from danger. It includes, but is not limited to, theater SAR; CSAR; SERE; evasion and recovery (E&R); and the coordination of negotiated as well as forcible recovery options.

b. Urban PR. All military personnel, including aviators, have the potential to become isolated. Recovery in an urban setting poses a unique challenge and can place a heavy demand on the isolated person(s), the recovery force, and operational planners tasked to return this individual to friendly control. Successful recovery of the isolated person, specifically the E&R component, may be predicated on overcoming a number of problems unique to an urban environment. With a higher indigenous population, the risk of immediate capture will be proportionally higher. It is also very likely that an evader in an urban setting will draw attention and thus be quickly cut off from friendly support. Therefore, individuals who can avoid immediate capture must be thoroughly familiar with urban evasion techniques. This is particularly important for aviators who, although trained in traditional evasion procedures (nonurban settings), are confronted with an unfamiliar environment. The challenges of urban evasion are mitigated through realistic training and a prepared evader. Training and preparation are also essential to a successful PR mission. Other critical elements include an effective C2 architecture and recovery force. A comprehensive understanding of urban evasion and recovery procedures is necessary because all elements of a joint force can be tasked to lend assistance in an urban PR mission.

c. Additional information is found in the following manuals; JP 3-50.2, Doctrine for Joint Combat Search and Rescue; JP 3-50.21, JTTP for Combat Search and Rescue, JP 3-50.3, Joint Doctrine for Evasion and Recovery; Air Force Doctrine Document (AFDD) 2-1.6, for CSAR, or AFTTP 3-1, Volumes 1, 3, 24, and 25 (Classified).

2. Evasion

a. Evasion skills. Urban evaders must be familiar with and skilled in movement and concealment techniques. The ability to use buildings, rubble, foliage, smoke, shadows, and sub-surface avenues will conceal movement and help avoid detection. Movement during the hours of darkness or low light conditions will also help minimize detection. Urban environments offer numerous areas to hide. Basements, subway tunnels, sewers, and other underground structures can offer suitable hideouts. Security during evasion movement may be enhanced by the use of specialized equipment, such as NVDs. These devices are also useful while conducting surveillance before attempting to move to a safer area and/or suitable recovery site.

b. Evader Movement. The absence of a nearby, suitable recovery site (e.g., HLZ) and/or the presence of hostile forces may require evader movement over a significant distance in order to link-up with friendly forces. Therefore, evaders must be able to precisely navigate and report their location. In an urban environment, traditional navigation skills may be degraded. Man-made structures will affect the evader's ability to take a straight route, visually acquire prominent landmarks, or view celestial navigational cues. Commercial hand-held GPS receivers provide specific position/location; however, their accuracy can yield position errors up to 150 meters, a margin that could equate to several city streets or blocks. An adequate GPS position may not be attainable in an urban environment due to satellite obscuration. Urban evaders will have to rely on major urban features including significant buildings, street names, and major intersections to provide specific location to recovery forces.

3. Charts, Communications, and Signaling

a. Charts, imagery, and landmarks. Standard 1:250,000 scale Evasion Charts (EVCs) may not provide sufficient detail to allow urban land or aerial navigation, especially in city centers. As such, providing aviators and recovery personnel with larger scale special purpose urban or high-resolution imagery are a priority consideration. Such charts and imagery can be difficult to obtain, but can greatly assist the mission planners in pinpointing the location of the evader before and during the recovery effort. During pre-mission study of urban environments, mission planners should identify significant (easily recognizable) landmarks and terrain features to serve as navigational reference points and as a means to determine location. Examples may include bridges, high-rise buildings, cathedrals, stadiums, major road intersections, or natural high ground (hilltops). Designate one selected feature or geoposition as the search and rescue dot (SARDOT). The SARDOT serves as a predesignated position from which evaders and recovery forces reference their current location. The evaders' position is transmitted relative in terms of radial/distance *from* the SARDOT. The (ATO) Special Instructions (SPINS) will include SARDOT location and specific instructions on how to use the SARDOT.

b. Communications. Communication presents another challenge for evaders. Currently fielded survival radios such as the PRC-90 and PRC-112 are non-secure and LOS limited. Urban terrain may block radio signals. In addition, radio transmissions can be intercepted and exploited by opposition forces. They may glean important information or find an evader's location using DF equipment and tactics. Although available in limited quantity (1000 units), the newly fielded PRC-112B (also called the HOOK 112) survival radio is a conventional PRC-112 modified with a GPS receiver. It is also upgraded with an encoded data burst capability that provides a covert or semi-secure means to communicate. (NOTE: Voice transmission over any of the five HOOK 112 frequencies is not secure. Only the data burst feature can be encoded for semi-secure communication.) Preprogrammed or free-text messages can be data burst transmitted and received. The PRC-112B data burst feature communicates with rescue forces through two specially designed airborne interrogation devices referred to as the SUITCASE Interrogator unit and QUICKDRAW unit. The QUICKDRAW, fielded only by the US Navy, is a less functional hand-held version of the SUITCASE Interrogator. The PRC-112B survival radio is affected by the same phenomenon and limitations of the standard issue PRC-90 and PRC-112 radios, including those associated with LOS and DF exploitation. Should the survival radio become unusable or inoperable, consider using existing communications systems. The commercial telephone system, if working, is one possibility that should not be overlooked. An international telephone credit card with emergency numbers as part of the aviator's personal evasion kit could simplify communicating via commercial telephone. Another option is the use of cellular telephones, some of which include secure capability as well as a worldwide coverage area. When all electronic means of voice communications fail, evaders will need to use visual electronic signals or construct a ground-to-air signal. These signals, that provide a recognizable contrast with the urban background, can be manmade items issued as survival equipment or improvised. Finally, Combat Survivor/Evader Locator (CSEL), if available, can provide two-way over-the-horizon secure message and voice communications; near real time geopositioning information between the user and a base station; and ability to identify/authenticate the specific user.

c. Signaling. Signaling methods should be pre-coordinated and documented in the individual's evasion plan of action (EPA). Furthermore, signaling devices and their employment must be commensurate with the environment in which they are used, be rapidly discernible by rescue forces, and avoid compromising the evader's location. To better facilitate the use of signaling devices, consider using equipment that is compact enough to be carried, easy to operate, and reusable. An urban environment presents clutter and light pollution when viewed from the air. Visually locating a lone evader in this situation can be difficult. Employing covert signaling devices developed specifically for day/night and vertical/horizontal application can overcome environmental limitations and allow the evader to become observable. The traditional signal mirror is visually observable at considerable distances and can be directed toward specific observers while concealed from unintended observers. However, careless use of this device can compromise an evader's location. Although less observable, another option is the visual signal (VS) -17 panel (NOTE: currently not carried by US Navy (USN) or USAF aviators). It is a brightly colored panel, which provides a bright color contrast when placed against a neutral background. A VS-17 panel, oriented vertically or horizontally, is generally easily recognized. Both the signal mirror and VS-17 panel should be used in accordance with the evasion plan of action to avoid unintended detection. Because the human eye can detect moving or blinking sources better than static or constant sources, careful consideration should be taken in night urban signaling: Visible light lasers such as a "Green Beam" work well. In addition, laser-pointing devices can be highly effective for signaling to NVG equipped recovery forces. They can also be used to illuminate/ designate targets or threats to the evader or recovery forces. (NOTE: In cases where laser-pointing devices are used, recovery package strike aircraft should use caution when engaging a target designated by an evader. The evader may not have the appropriate training/familiarity to perform target designation duties.) Another signaling device is the FIREFLY. Fireflies are IR light emitting diodes, powered by a 9-volt direct current (DC) battery. They are employed in two methods, either in the factory setting mode or in a programmable mode. Each mode dictates the sequence and frequency of the flash. The programmable model has a unique coding system, which allows any sequence of flashes up to four seconds in duration, to be programmed into the unit. The advantage of the programmable model is the ability to code beacons with different flash rates, enabling any one to be distinguished from a group. Either model provides an effective method of attracting attention of friendly forces. Equipped with several Fireflies, an evader can attach the lights to a length of string and display them from a window or rooftop for observation by recovery forces. Again, the best employment of this device will result from a comprehensive scheme outlined in the individual's EPA. Glint tape or other combat identification systems can facilitate distinct identification of evaders. In addition, "No Power Thermal Target Material" known as "cold sky" can enhance evader recognition to friendly FLIR/IDS-equipped aircraft. Certain environments may permit the use of overt signals such as smoke grenades, flares, penguns, and personal locator beacons (that emit homing signals) regardless of day/night conditions to assist recovery operations. However, employment of these devices must be measured against the potential for unintended compromise of the evader's position and added danger to recovery forces.

4. Recovery

Urban recovery may increase the intelligence requirements for a successful recovery. Knowing the evader's exact location is an essential element that significantly reduces recovery force exposure time during the terminal phase of a recovery mission. Depending on threat assessments and vulnerabilities, time available to search for the evader may be limited. Consider incorporating a concept of operations to employ UAVs to locate an evader. Equipping evaders with the latest technology in navigation and signaling devices improves the evader's chances for swift and successful recovery. Evasion and recovery plans must be carefully crafted, briefed and fully understood.

REFERENCES

Joint

1. Joint Pub 1-02, *DOD Dictionary of Military and Associated Terms*, As amended through 10 January 2000.
2. Joint Pub 3-09.3, *JTTP for Close Air Support (CAS)*, 1 December 1995.
3. Joint Pub 3-50.21, *JTTP for Combat Search and Rescue*, 23 March 1998.
4. Joint Pub 3-50.3, *Joint Doctrine for Evasion and Recovery*, 6 September 1996.
5. Joint Pub 3-56.1, *Command and Control for Joint Air Operations*, 14 November 1994.

Multi-Service

1. The *Air Land Sea Bulletin (ALSB) 96-1*, article on "AC-130 Gunship CAS" written by Capt Havel, 18th Flight Test Squadron (FTS).
2. The *ALSB 97-3*, article on "AC-130 Employment during MOUT" written by Capt Taylor, HQ Air Force Special Operations Command (AFSOC/DOVF, Flight Standards Branch).

Army

1. FM 90-10, *Military Operations on Urbanized Terrain (MOUT)*, 15 August 1979.
2. FM 90-10-1, *An Infantryman's Guide to Combat in Built-up Areas*, 12 May 1993.
3. FM 1-100, *Army Aviation Operations*, 21 Feb 1997.
4. FM 1-111, *Aviation Brigades*, 27 Oct 1997.
5. FM 1-112, *Attack Helicopter Operations*, 02 Apr 1997.
6. FM 1-113, *Utility and Cargo Helicopter Operations*, 12 Sep 1997.
7. FM 1-120, *Army Air Traffic Services Contingency and Combat Zone Operations*, 22 May 1995.
8. FM 1-140, *Helicopter Gunnery*, 29 Mar 1996.
9. FM 5-33, *Terrain Analysis*, 11 Jul 1990.
10. FM 34-130, *Intelligence Preparation of the Battlefield*, 08 Jul 1994.
11. FM 100-5, *Operations*, 14 Jun 1993.
12. FM 100-103, *Army Airspace Command and Control in a Combat Zone*, 07 Oct 1987.
13. FM 100-103-1, *Integrated Combat Airspace Command and Control (ICAC2)*, 03 Oct 1994.
14. TC 1-209, *Aircrew Training Manual, Aviator/Aeroscout Observer, OH-58D*, 09 Dec 1992.
15. TC 1-211, *Aircrew Training Manual, Utility Helicopter, UH-1*, 09 Dec 1992.
16. TC 1-212, *Aircrew Training Manual, Utility Helicopter, UH-60/EH-60*, 08 Mar 1996.
17. TC 1-213, *Aircrew Training Manual, Attack Helicopter, AH-1*, 09 Dec 1992.
18. TC 1-214, *Aircrew Training Manual, Attack Helicopter, AH-64*, 20 May 1992.
19. TC 1-215, *Aircrew Training Manual, Observation Helicopter, OH-58-A/C*, 02 Mar 1993.
20. TC 1-216, *Aircrew Training Manual, Cargo Helicopter, CH-47*, 08 Oct 1992.
21. CALL Newsletter 90-9, *Operation JUST CAUSE (Vols I, II, III)*.
22. CALL Newsletter 93-7, *Operations Other Than War Volume III, Civil Disturbance*.
23. CALL Lessons Learned Report, *US Army Operations in Support of UNOSOM II*.

24. CALL Bulletin 90-4, *Introduction to Low Intensity Conflict.*
25. CALL Handbook 92-3, *Fratricide Risk Assessment for Company Leadership.*
26. CALL Newsletter 92-4, *Fratricide: Reducing Self-Inflicted Losses.*
27. CALL Newsletter 94-3, *(Special Edition) Haiti.*
28. CALL Newsletter 93-1, *(Special Edition) Somalia.*
29. CALL Newsletter 95-13, *(Special Edition) Supporting the Peace: Bosnia-Herzegovina.*

Marine Corps

1. MCWP 3-35.3, *Military Operations on Urbanized Terrain (MOUT)*, 16 April 1998.
2. *Aviation Combat Element Military Operations on Urban Terrain Manual*, edition VI, December 1997.

Navy

1. *Naval Institute Proceedings*, February 1998, "MOUT: The Show Stopper" written by Robert E. Polesny.
2. *Navy Times Marine Corps Edition*, February 16, 1998, "Urban Warriors" written by John R. Anderson.
3. *Navy Aviation Systems Team Handbook AVDEP-HDBK-12, Mapping, Charting, and Geodesy.*

Air Force

AFDD 1, *Air Force Basic Doctrine*, 1 Sep 1997.
AFDD 2-1, *Air Warfare*, 22 Jan 2000.
AFDD 2-1.3, *Counterland*, 27 Aug 1999.
AFDD 2-1.6, *Combat Search, and Rescue*, 30 Sep 1998.
AFDD 2-1.7, *Airspace Control in the Combat Zone*, 4 Jun 1998.
AFDD 2-3, *Military Operations Other Than War (MOOTW)*, 5 Oct 1996.
AFDD 2-6, *Air Mobility Operations*, 13 Nov 1999.
AFDD 2-6.1, *Airlift Operations*, 13 Nov 1999.
AFDD 2-7, *Special Operations*, 1 Jul 1999.
AFTTP 3-1, *Series Publications.*
422 TES April 1998 Final Report, Urban Close Air Support Tactics, Development, and Evaluation (S).
Article: Mission Planning for Rescue Operations in Urban Terrain (ROUT), by Capt Michael D. Geragosian, 422 TES/DOH.

Other

1. Rand Note N-3519-AF, *Air Force Noncombat Operations: Lessons from the Past, Thoughts for the Future.*
2. Rand Report R-1871-ARPA, *Military Operations in Built-Up Areas: Essays on Some Past, Present, and Future Aspects.*
3. DMA Homepage, http://www.dma.gov
4. NOAA Homepage, http://www.noaa.gov
5. USGS Homepage, http://www.usgs.gov
6. TEC Mosaic Homepage, http//cat.tec.army.mil/

7. Real-Time Support for the Warrior, http://www.ait.nrl.navy.mil/rts/warrior.html

8. 61 JTCG/ME-1-2, *Joint Service Index of Specialized Technical Handbooks* (U)

9. 61 JTCG/ME-87-1, *Initial Development/Application of Urban Terrain Data for Artillery Employment in MOUT* (U)

10. 61 JTCG/ME-88-7, *JMEM/AS Weaponeering Guide* (U)

Glossary

PART I—ABBREVIATIONS AND ACRONYMS

A

AA	assembly areas
AAA	antiaircraft artillery
ABCCC	airborne battlefield command and control center
ACA	airspace coordination area
ACP	air control point
AFDC	Air Force Doctrine Center
AFDD	Air Force Doctrine Document
AFI	Air Force Instruction
AFTTP	Air Force Tactics, Techniques, and Procedures
AFTTP(I)	Air Force Tactics, Techniques, and Procedures (Interservice)
AGL	above ground level
AGM	air-to-surface guided missile
AIE	alternate insertion/extraction
ALSA	Air Land Sea Application
ALLTV	all light level television
AP	armor piercing
APC	armored personnel carrier
API	armor piercing incendiary
APT	armor piercing tracer
ASE	aircraft survivability equipment
ATC	air traffic control
ATO	air tasking order
AWACS	Airborne Warning and Control System

B

BDA	battle damage assessment
BLU	bomb live unit
BPS	basic PSYOP study
BTG	basic targeting graphic
BTO	battle tracking overlay

C

C2	command and control
C3	command, control, and communications
CA	civil affairs
CARVER	criticality, accessibility, recuperability, vulnerability, effect, recognizability
CAS	close air support
CATF	Commander, Amphibious Task Force
CBU	cluster bomb unit

CCDTV	charged coupled device television
CDET	collateral damage estimate tool
CEP	circular error probable
CEM	combined effects munition
CJCS	Chairman of the Joint Chiefs of Staff
CJCSI	CJCS Instruction
cm	centimeter
COA	course of action
COO	combined obstacle overlay
CSAR	combat search and rescue
CSEL	combat survivor evader locator
CSP	contingency support package
CSS	contingency support study

D

DA	Department of Army
DALS	downed aviator locator system (USN)
DC	direct current
DCA	defensive counter-air
DF	direction finding
DFAD	digital feature analysis data
DIA	Defense Intelligence Agency
DMA	Defense Mapping Agency
DMPI	desired mean point of impact
DOD	Department of Defense
DOS	Department of State
DSN	Defense Switched Network
DTAMS	digital terrain analysis mapping system
DTED	digital terrain elevation data
DTSS	digital topographic support system
DTV	day television
DVO	Direct View Optics
DZ	drop zone

E

E&R	evasion & recovery
EAP	emergency action plan
EO	electro-optical
ELINT	electronic intelligence
EPA	evasion plan of action
EVC	evasion chart

F

FAC	forward air controller
FAC (A)	forward air controller airborne
FAE	fuel-air explosive

FARP	forward arming and refueling point
FHM	flight hazard map
FID	feature identification
FLIP	Flight Information Publication, flight instruction procedures
FLIR	forward-looking infrared
FM	field manual
FMU	fused munition unit
FSE	fire support element

G

GBU	guided bomb unit
GLINT	gated laser intensifier
GP	general purpose
GPS	global positioning system
GRG	gridded reference graphic

H

HARM	high-speed anti-radiation missile
HE	high explosive
HEAT	high explosive, anti-tank
HEI	high explosive incendiary
HEI-P	high explosive incendiary-plugged
HE-P	high explosive-plugged
HEDP	high explosive dual purpose
HIDACZ	high-density airspace control zone
HLZ	helicopter landing zone
HN	host nation
HTS	HARM targeting system
HUMINT	human intelligence

I

IADS	integrated air defense system
ICAC2	integrated combat airspace command and control
ID	identification
IDF	Israel Defense Forces
IDM	improved data modem
IDS	integrated display system
IFF	identification, friend or foe
INS	inertial navigation system
INTELINK	Intelligence Link
IO	information operations
IP	initial point
IPB	intelligence preparation of the battlespace
IR	infrared
ISP ISR	intelligence support package Intelligence, Surveillance, Reconaissance

IZLID	Infrared Zoom Laser Illuminator Designator

J

JACC/CP	joint airborne communications center/command post
JARSP	Joint annual review of SERE production
JDAM	Joint Direct Attack Munition
JDISS	Joint deployable intelligence support system
JFC	Joint force commander
JIPB	Joint intelligence preparation of the battlespace
JMEM	Joint Munitions Effectiveness Manual
JOG	Joint operations graphics
JP	Joint publication
JSSA	Joint Services SERE Agency
JSTARS	joint surveillance, target, attack, radar system
JTF	Joint task force
JWAC	Joint Warfare Assessment Center

K

km	kilometer

L

LANDSAT	land satellite
LGB	laser guided bomb
LLLTV	low-light level television
LOAC	law of armed conflict
LOC	line of communications
LOS	line of sight
LPL	laser pointer long range
LST	laser spot tracker
LTD	laser target designator
LTD/R	laser target designator/ranger
LUU	
LZ	landing zone

M

m	meter
MAGTF	Marine air-ground task force
MANPADS	man-portable air defense system
MAWTS-1	Marine Aviation Weapons and Tactics Squadron One
MCCDC	Marine Corps Combat Development Command
MCIA	Marine Corps Intelligence Activity
MCPDS	Marine Corps publication distribution system
MCRP	Marine Corps reference publication
MCS	military capabilities study
MCOO	modified combined obstacle overlay

MEDEVAC	medical evacuation
MEU	Marine expeditionary unit
MGRS	Military Grid Reference System
MILSTRIP	military standard requisitioning and issue procedure
Mk	mark
mm	millimeter
MOUT	military operations on urbanized terrain
MRE	meal, ready to eat
MSL	mean sea level
MTTP	multi-Service tactics, techniques, and procedures

N

NAS	Naval air station
NAVSOP	Naval standing operating procedure
NCA	National Command Authorities
NEO	noncombatant evacuation operation
NISH	NEO intelligence support handbook
NEOPAC	noncombatant evacuation operation packet
NFA	no-fire area
NGIC	National Ground Intelligence Center
NGO	nongovernmental organization
NIIRS	national imagery interpretability rating scale
NIMA	National Imagery and Mapping Agency
NSFS	naval surface fire support
NSWC	Naval Strike Warfare Center
NTM	national technical means
NVD	night vision devices
NVG	night vision goggles
NWDC	Navy Warfare Development Command

O

OCA	offensive counter-air
OPLAN	operations plan
OPORD	operations order
OPR	office of primary responsibility

P

PD	point detonating
PGM	precision-guided munitions
PGU	precision guidance unit
Pi	probability of incapacitation
PPN	
PR	personnel recovery
psi	pounds per square inch
PSYOP	psychological operations
PZ	pickup zone

Q

R

Rds	rounds
RFI	request for information
RHA	rolled homogenous armor
ROE	rules of engagement
ROZ	restricted operating zone

S

SAID	safe area intelligence description
SAM	surface-to-air missile
SAR	search and rescue
SARDOT	search and rescue dot
SEAD	suppression of enemy air defense
SERE	survival, evasion, resistance, and escape
SFW	sensor-fuzed weapon
SLAM	stand-off land attack missile
SOCRATES	Special Operations Command Research, Analysis and Threat Evaluation System
SOF	special operations forces
SOP	standing operating procedure
SPA	special PSYOP assessment
SPINS	special instructions
SPS	special PSYOP study
SROE	standing rules of engagement
SSD	strategic studies detachment
SST	selectable strike

T

TACP	tactical air control party
TGP	targeting pod
TIC	troops in contact
TLM	tactical land maps
TNT	trinitrotoluene
TOW	tube launched, optically tracked, wire guided
TP	training projectile
TPC	tactical pilotage chart
TRADOC	Training and Doctrine Command
TRAP	tactical recovery of aircraft and personnel
TRP	target reference point
TTP	tactics, techniques, and procedures
TV/EO	television/electro-optical

U

UARM	unconventional assisted recovery mechanism
UAV	unmanned aerial vehicle
UCMJ	uniform code of military justice
US	United States
USAF	United States Air Force
USMC	United States Marine Corps
USN	United States Navy
UTFO	urban terrain feature overlay
UTM	universal transverse mercator
UTOG	urban terrain orientation graphic

V

VAP	visible area plots
VHS	video home system
VIRS	visually initiated release system
VS	visual signal
VSP	video support product
VT	variable time

W

WEZ	weapons engagement zone
WGS	World Geodetic System
WP	white phosphorus

X

Y

Z

PART II—TERMS AND DEFINITIONS

call for fire (DOD, NATO). A request for fire containing data necessary for obtaining the required fire on a target.

close air support (DOD). Air action by fixed- and rotary-wing aircraft against hostile targets which are in close proximity to friendly forces and which require detailed integration of each air mission with the fire and movement of those forces. Also called CAS.

cluster bomb unit (DOD, NATO). An aircraft store composed of a dispenser and submunitions.

combat search and rescue (DOD). A specific task performed by rescue forces to effect the recovery of distressed personnel during war or military operations other than war. Also called CSAR.

control point (DOD, NATO). 1. A position along a route of march at which men are stationed to give information and instructions for the regulation of supply or traffic. 2. A position marked by a buoy, boat, aircraft, electronic device, conspicuous terrain feature, or other identifiable object which is given a name or number and used as an aid to navigation or control of ships, boats, or aircraft. 3. In making mosaics, a point located by ground survey with which a corresponding point on a photograph is matched as a check.

danger close (DOD, NATO). In artillery and naval gunfire support, information in a call for fire to indicate that friendly forces are within 600 meters of the target.

datum (geodetic) (DOD). A reference surface consisting of five quantities: the latitude and longitude of an initial point, the azimuth of a line from that point, and the parameters of the reference ellipsoid.

direct fire (DOD). Gunfire delivered on a target, using the target itself as a point of aim for either the gun or the director.

direct supporting fire (DOD, NATO). Fire delivered in support of part of a force, as opposed to general supporting fire which is delivered in support of the force as a whole.

drop zone (DOD, NATO). A specific area upon which airborne troops, equipment, or supplies are airdropped.

evasion and recovery (DOD). the full spectrum of coordinated actions carried out by evader, recovery forces, and operational recovery planners to effect the successful repatriation of personnel isolated in hostile territory to friendly control. (JP 3-50.3) This method includes, but is not limited to, recovery by surface craft, submarines, SOF aircraft or ground / sea teams, and unconventional assisted recovery mechanism (UARM).

fire support (DOD). Fires that directly support land, maritime, amphibious, and special operation forces to engage enemy forces, combat formations, and facilities in pursuit of tactical and operational objectives.

forward looking infrared (DOD). An airborne, electro-optical thermal imaging device that detects far-infrared energy, converts the energy into an electronic signal, and provides a visible image for day or night viewing. Also called FLIR.

helicopter landing zone (DOD). A specified ground area for landing assault helicopters to embark or disembark troops and/or cargo. A landing zone may contain one or more landing sites.

high-density airspace control zone (DOD). Airspace designated in an airspace control plan or airspace control order, in which there is a concentrated employment of numerous and varied weapons and airspace users. A high-density airspace control zone has defined dimensions, which usually coincide with geographical features or navigational aids. Access to a high-density airspace control zone is normally controlled by the maneuver commander. The maneuver commander can also direct a more restrictive weapons status within the high-density airspace control zone. Also called HIDACZ.

holding point (DOD). A geographically or electronically defined location used in stationing aircraft in flight in a predetermined pattern in accordance with ATC clearance.

joint fires (DOD). Fires produced during the employment of forces from two or more components in coordinated action toward a common objective.

Joint Munitions Effectiveness Manual (DOD). A publication providing a single, comprehensive source of information covering weapon effectiveness, selection, and requirements for special operations munitions. In addition, the closely related fields of weapon characteristics and effects, target characteristics, and target vulnerability are treated in limited detail required by the mission planner. Although emphasis is placed on weapons that are currently in the inventory, information is also included for some weapons not immediately available but projected for the near future. Also called JMEM.

joint urban operations (DOD). Joint operations planned and conducted across the range of military operations on, or against objectives on, a topographical complex and its adjacent natural terrain where manmade construction and the density of noncombatants are the dominant features. Also called JUO.

landing zone (DOD, NATO). Any specified zone used for the landing of aircraft.

military grid reference system (DOD, NATO). A system which uses a standard-scaled grid square, based on a point of origin on a map projection of the surface of the earth in an accurate and consistent manner to permit either position referencing or the computation of direction and distance between grid positions.

military operations on urbanized terrain. All military actions that are planned and conducted on a topographical complex and its adjacent natural terrain where manmade construction is the dominant feature. It includes combat in cities, which is that portion of combat involving house-to-house and street-by-street fighting in towns and cities. Also called MOUT.

night vision device (DOD). Any electro-optical device that is used to detect visible and infrared energy and provide a visible image. Night vision goggles, forward-looking infrared, thermal sights, and low light level television are night vision devices. Also called NVD.

night vision goggle(s) (DOD). An electro-optical image intensifying device that detects visible and near-infrared energy, intensifies the energy, and provides a visible image for night viewing. Night vision goggles can be either hand-held or helmet-mounted. Also called NVG.

noncombatant evacuation operations (DOD). Operations directed by the Department of State, the Department of Defense, or other appropriate authority whereby noncombatants are evacuated from foreign countries when their lives are endangered by war, civil unrest, or natural disaster to safe havens or to the United States. Also called NEO.

nongovernmental organizations (DOD). Transnational organizations of private citizens that maintain a consultative status with the Economic and Social Council of the United Nations. Nongovernmental organizations may be professional associations, foundations, multinational businesses, or simply groups with a common interest in humanitarian assistance activities (development and relief). "Nongovernmental organizations" is a term normally used by non-United States organizations. Also called NGO.

personnel recovery (DOD). The umbrella term for operations focused on the task of recovering captured, missing, or isolated personnel from danger. It is the sum of military, civil, and political efforts to obtain the release or recovery of personnel from uncertain or hostile environments and denied areas either they are captured, missing, or isolated. That includes US, allied, coalition, friendly military, or paramilitary and others designated by the National Command Authorities (NCA). PR includes, but is not limited to, theater (civil) search and rescue (SAR); combat search and rescue (CSAR); survival, evasion, resistance, and escape (SERE); evasion and recovery (E&R); and the coordination of negotiated as well as forcible recovery options. PR may occur through military action, action by nongovernmental organizations (NGO), other US Government-approved action, and/or diplomatic initiatives, or through any of those options. Also called PR.

positive control (DOD). A method of airspace control which relies on positive identification, tracking, and direction of aircraft within an airspace, conducted with electronic means by an agency having the authority and responsibility therein.

precision bombing (DOD). Bombing directed at a specific point target.

rules of engagement (DOD). Directives issued by competent military authority which delineate the circumstances and limitations under which United States forces will initiate and/or continue combat engagement with other forces encountered. Also called ROE.

SARDOT. A reference point on land that serves as a predesignated position from which evaders and recovery forces reference their current location. The Air Tasking Order (ATO) Special Instructions (SPINS) will include SARDOT location and specific instructions on how to use the SARDOT.

target (DOD). 1. A geographical area, complex, or installation planned for capture or destruction by military forces. 2. In intelligence usage, a country, area, installation, agency, or person against which intelligence operations are directed. 3. An area designated and numbered for future firing. 4. In gunfire support usage, an impact burst which hits the target.

targeting (DOD). 1. The process of selecting targets and matching the appropriate response to them, taking account of operational requirements and capabilities. 2. The analysis of enemy situations relative to the commander's mission, objectives, and capabilities at the commander's disposal, to identify and nominate specific vulnerabilities that, if exploited, will accomplish the commander's purpose through delaying, disrupting, disabling, or destroying enemy forces or resources critical to the enemy.

universal transverse mercator grid (DOD, NATO). A grid coordinate system based on the transverse mercator projection, applied to maps of the Earth's surface extending to 84 degrees N and 80 degrees S latitudes. Also called UTM Grid.

INDEX

V

W

FM 3-06.1
MCRP 3-35.3A
NTTP 3-01.04
AFTTP(I) 3-2.29
15 April 2001

By Order of the Secretary of the Army:

Official:

ERIC K. SHINSEKI
General, United States Army
Chief of Staff

JOEL B. HUDSON
Administrative Assistant to the
Secretary of the Army

DISTRIBUTION:
Active Army, Army National Guard, and U.S. Army Reserve: Distribute in
accordance with the initial distribution number (IDN) 115847
requirements for FM 3-06.1.

By Order of the Secretary of the Air Force:

LANCE L. SMITH
Major General, USAF
Commander
Headquarters Air Force Doctrine Center

Air Force Distribution: F

www.ingramcontent.com/pod-product-compliance
Lightning Source LLC
Chambersburg PA
CBHW081106290526
45795CB00006B/2023